WHAT TO DO WHEN EVERYONE'S DOING IT

Moral Messages From
A College Chapel

BY HAROLD C. WARLICK, JR.

C.S.S Publishing Co., Inc.
Lima, Ohio

WHAT TO DO WHEN EVERYONE'S DOING IT

Copyright © 1992 by
The C.S.S. Publishing Company, Inc.
Lima, Ohio

All rights reserved. No part of this publication may be reproduced, stored in a retrieval system, or transmitted in any form or by any means, electronic, mechanical, photocopying, recording, or otherwise, without the prior permission of the publisher. Inquiries should be addressed to: The C.S.S. Publishing Company, Inc., 628 South Main Street, Lima, Ohio 45804.

Library of Congress Cataloging-in-Publication Data

Warlick, Harold C.
    What to do when everyone's doing it : moral messages from a college chapel / by Harold C. Warlick.
      p.   cm.
    ISBN 1-55673-409-3
    1. Youth sermons.   2. Sermons, American.   I. Title.
BV4310.W355   1992
252'.55—dc20   91-30631
                                                                                      CIP

9222 / ISBN 1-55673-409-3   PRINTED IN U.S.A.

Dedicated to Charles and Pauline Hayworth in appreciation for their concern, support, and affirmation.

Table Of Contents

I. What To Do When Everyone's Doing It
- What To Do When Everyone's Doing It — 9
- Being Different — 15
- Living Life The Easy Way — 23
- Power — 29
- Real Strength — 37

II. Belief And Behavior
- Compassion — 45
- The Cracking Point — 53
- The Necessity Of Forgiveness — 61
- The Housing Problem — 67
- The World's Best Kept Secret — 73

III. Survival And The Self
- Coping With Anger In A Close-up World — 81
- Repairing Your Broken Dreams — 87
- Don't Give Up Too Soon! — 93
- Wheels Instead Of Walls — 99
- The Shortest Distance Is Not A Straight Line — 105

What To Do When Everyone's Doing It

What To Do When
Everyone's Doing It
Being Different
Living Life The Easy Way
Power
Real Strength

What To Do When Everyone's Doing It

Judges 6:25-31
Romans 12:1-2

I harbor few illusions that people take to heart sermons like I'm about to preach. Yet later on in life we just might look back and remember. W. T. Leitze taught me that very early in life. W. T. Leitze was one of the kindest, most trusting individuals who ever lived. Mr. Leitze, a 60-year-old bachelor who weighed at least 300 pounds, was my ninth grade algebra teacher. Mr. Leitze's whole life was centered around his students. His lectures always interwove basic algebraic principles with basic Christian morals. He had abiding faith in his students and could move a class of 15-year-old boys and girls to tears as he voiced his dreams for the contributions that class could make to society.

Well, one Friday morning Mr. Leitze walked into the algebra class a little late. As he stood by his desk and glanced around the room, he raised his eyebrows in surprise. The bottom part of the huge pencil sharpener, the part that catches the shavings, was gone. Mr. Leitze told everyone to look at the pencil sharpener, and all eyes turned to the side of the big wooden cabinet where the main body of the sharpener was bolted. "It seems that someone has forgotten to return the bottom part of the sharpener to its rightful place," he began. "Knowing this fine, upstanding, honest group of young people as I do," he continued, "I know that it is just a matter of forgetfulness."

Then Mr. Leitze went on: "We don't want to embarrass that person, who I know wants to return it, so here's what we'll do. Each person, beginning with me, will place his and her head down on the desk and close his eyes. No one will look.

I forbid it. And the person who forgot to return it can get out of his seat and take it back."

Well, when Mr. Leitze spoke, one did as he instructed. So Mr. Leitze placed his big ole head down on his massive arms and closed his eyes. The rest of the class did the same. After a few seconds, a pair of feet hit the floor and you could hear them shuffling back toward the wooden cabinet. I smiled to myself at the honesty of a classmate. It wasn't one of the three most logical candidates, three football players, because Mr. Leitze seated everyone in alphabetical order and the shuffling came from a different part of the room from where Warlick, Wiggins and Zier were seated.

Presently, we heard some rattling and noise from the area of the pencil sharpener. Then the same shuffling feet returned to the area from which they had come, and all was silent. Mr. Leitze broke the silence. "All right, children, I'm proud of you," he boomed. Almost in unison Mr. Leitze and 30 pairs of eyes looked up and turned to the wooden cabinet. The whole sharpener was gone. Somebody had taken the rest of the mechanism. There were four holes in the cabinet and the outline of where the pencil sharpener had been.

The whole room was mesmerized. Mr. Leitze put his head down on the desk and started crying. When he did not stop, one of the girls ran and got the principal. The principal came rushing into the room. "For God's sake, Leitze, what did you expect them to do?" he roared.

I'm more realistic than W. T. Leitze. I don't expect massive change. But I do have hope for some change on our campus and some change in the world.

It's been said that the degree, B.A., stands for bachelor of abilities. To some degree it might. I know that whenever rationale is summoned for questionable behavior, the first line of defense is the alibi: but everybody is doing it. In fact, talk to some people and you get the opinion that everyone is drinking to excess; everyone is sexually active; everyone is cheating; everyone is bending the rules.

I've often wondered about that. If it's so wonderful and indeed, everybody is doing it, why do they have to pressure you into doing it? Did you ever think of that? If everybody is really doing it, why do they need you and me to do it?

In our world, if you have to live by one rule, live by this one: respect the customs of others but not at the expense of your own values.

One of the most poignant passages of Scripture is the 12th chapter of Paul's letter to the church in Rome. J. B. Phillips translates it in these words: *"Don't let the world around you squeeze you into its mold."* Renew your own mind and do that which is good and perfect. In other words, you may have to live in a crowd, but you do not have to live like it. That is hard to do in an age of conformity, isn't it? It is difficult to stand as a minority with different values, different use of money, and a different language in our world. Such is perhaps the biggest problem a young person faces in growing to adulthood in a world of casual sex, easy drugs and infatuation with economic and material success. It is easy to be brave when everyone agrees with you; but the difficulty comes when you have to stand out, one among many, remembering your obligations as a child of God. It is just as difficult for adults. It takes some real effort to live a good life in today's world. More people are selfish than are generous. More people stay home in the dorm or elsewhere tonight than come to worship. More people have shaky marriages than strong ones. More people spend less time on their children than in personal pursuits than people who reverse that process. Ah, but it is difficult not to let the world squeeze you into its mold. It is difficult being in the minority. And it doesn't get any easier the older you get. It gets harder because you have more to lose.

For most of my life, the one Scripture verse that had the most practicaal application was Romans 12:2 — "Don't let the world squeeze you into its mold, but renew your own mind and do that which is good." I memorized that as a teenager and I had to really hold to that in many situations in life. Frankly, I used to go to my dormitory room in college and read that in the Bible many a night. I must have underlined it in a dozen different colors of ink. You see, I played football in college and even way back then college athletics was something else. I mean, the majority of college football players do not go to the library every night and study. And there was always the man who came by after victory with ten $20 bills rolled up in his fist and said, "Nice game," as he stuck one in your pocket. The majority did not say, "No, thank you. We're not allowed to take that." There was always the restaurant owner who knew all the players and winked as he said, "Drink all you want; the tab's on me." The majority did not say, "No, thank you" or "One is enough." And drugs. Even then, we had six or seven guys who could have opened a pharmacy. The fraternities were mild in comparison to today's, but even then at our SAE parties, it was still the minority posture to say "no, thank you" to many things.

When you hear or read about a decision handed down by our Supreme Court, the name is announced of the justice who wrote the minority report. Interestingly enough, if you wish to view most of what is now majority law or majority action in our country, you could go through the past four decades of decisions and read the minority reports. Most of the good causes in our way of life began with a minority and grew until they reached a majority. In fact, when our country began, only one-third of the people really wanted independence. The "best" two-thirds in the colonies said, "You are crazy to try to fight Great Britain with a few amateurs." They were a crazy minority, indeed.

One of the craziest minority reports is chronicled in the sixth chapter of Judges. It seems that the majority of the people in that culture worshiped a strange god named Baal. Baal was the pagan fertility god, so the people had erected a huge altar to him. Well, an angel of the Lord God came to Gideon and told Gideon to make a minority report. Gideon was to take his father's strongest bull, one that was seven years old, and hitch it up to the altar of Baal and pull it down. And while he was at it, he might as well cut down the sacred pole the people worshiped, and burn it. So, Gideon took ten men and one night they sneaked out and hitched up the bull and pulled down the altar to Baal, and burned the sacred pole. You can just imagine the furor that took place the next morning. Everyone in town woke up and knew what had happened. It didn't take them long to find out that Gideon had done it. The whole town came marching down to Gideon's house with blood in their eyes.

Gideon's father, Joash, went to the front door. The crowd yelled, "Bring out your son that he may die. He has pulled down the altar of Baal and burned the sacred trees next to it."

Joash stood before the crowd and said, "Wait a minute, let me get this straight. You are having to defend your god against one little man. Your god is so weak he needs you to protect him from one little man? You have to plead for the god of the majority of the people? Let Baal take care of himself. If he is so great, let him plead for himself because one little minority person has pulled down his altar."

That seemed to make sense to the people. From that day on they called Gideon, Jerubbaal, which means, "Let Baal take care of himself if he can."

I repeat: If everybody's doing it, and it's so great and powerful, why can't it take care of itself? Why do they try to pressure you and me into doing it? Is it so superficial, so weak, and so fake that it has to pressure someone into doing it, too?

Finally, consider this. There are some things that are so destructive that the only way you can be a success is not to engage in them at all.

In the movie *War Games*, a scientist built a marvelous computer named Joshua. Into this computer were placed all the responses and counter-responses the American defense system could make in a nuclear war. A child accidentally gained access to Joshua and started playing thermonuclear global war. Joshua, of course, did not know it was just a game. Joshua assumed total control over military weapons, and even the generals and scientists could not shut him down. Fortunately the builder of Joshua had created him with the capacity to learn from the consequences and moves of the game. Joshua began to accelerate his responses, projecting deaths on both sides from nuclear missiles and fall-out until the computer rapidly tallied up the losses for each side. Finally, Joshua shut itself off with the statement — *"Strange game; the only way to win is not to play."*

There are some strange games we play in life. The only way for an alcoholic to win at the game of drinking is to not play the game. The only way for a gambler to win at gambling is to not play the game. The only way for a married person to win at the game of having an affair is to not have one. The only way for a teenage girl and boy to win at the game of going to the beach with a six-pack and a blanket is to not play the game. The only way for a father to win at the game of concurrently seeking undue wealth, vengeance on his enemies, personal gratification and accomplished parenthood is not to play that game.

From personal experience I can tell you that the only surefire way to quit smoking is not to smoke in the first place.

All of us have to learn what not to do in life. What do you do when everyone's doing it?

Being Different
Daniel 3:1-18
John 17:13-19
Acts 5:29

You can learn something from a hurricane. I've noticed that the trees which tended to survive the onslaught of Hurricane Hugo were those which leaned against the wind. Most of the trees that were leaning with the wind were snapped in two or blown up by their roots.

Students need to be challenged to occasionally lean against the wind. All people occasionally need to lean against the wind. This isn't easy in a world like ours. The mass media begins training children to be consumers before they are three years old. Before you are three, people have been working to try to get you to buy what the crowd buys.

When I was an infant, barely able to talk, a relative would grab my foot and start pulling the toes from big toe around to little toe. She'd say, "This little piggy went to market. This little piggy stayed home. This little piggy had roast beef. This little piggy had none."

Then, with great fanfare, she would grab my little toe and screech, "And this little piggy went 'we-we-we' all the way home." And I'd just laugh.

Today, I'm afraid that wouldn't work. The children wouldn't understand. The little pigs all go to market, none stays home; all have roast beef, and all say "we-we-we."[1]

It's a lonely business to be out of step with the crowd. Many a person will throw away all his ideas, ideals and knowledge, simply to feel like "one of the boys" or "one of the girls." There's something nice about belonging to an easy, comfortable group whose talk reaches no higher than money and the opposite sex or the upcoming party. People will do anything for that kind of security. Many a person has stood on the brink of crisis and uttered those tragic words, "but everybody was doing it, and I was pressured to try it, too."

The Bible contains a story of three people who did not mind being different, even in the face of death. A certain king east of the Suez had just won a notable victory over his enemies. He wanted to celebrate. He set up a golden image, most probably a statue of Zeus, which was 90 feet high, roughly the height of our steeple. In front of the statue he built a huge altar on which pigs would be sacrificed. This was your ultimate political pig-picking party. He hired a great orchestra — cornets, bagpipes, flutes, dulcimers, drums and harps. They could play all kinds of music. And all the people were commanded to fall down and worship this monument to the king's ego when the band played the mid-East version of "Hail to the Chief" or "God Save the Queen" or the "National Anthem." All the politicians were there — the princes, the governors, the bankers, the judges, the lawyers, the doctors, the school board, the city council, the sheriffs and the mayors. Imagine the significance of the crowd. Anybody who was anybody was there.

Buoyed by such a show of support, if not affection, the victorious king was really feeling his oats: such a public mandate. Consequently he made the stimulating announcement that anyone who did not fall down in front of the idol would be cast into a furnace of fire.

Well, the expedient thing to do was to make the proper gesture, lick the king's boots and bow down. You know, when in Rome do as the Romans do.

There were three men who refused to follow the crowd. They refused to bend their knees to the false god. These men possessed rather odd names — Shadrach, Meshach and Abednego. When all those Babylonians hit their knees before that pagan god, they stood erect.

Obviously, such display of resistance bothered the king. It enraged him. He not only examined these who dared be different, but he set up the clash of the story with his rhetorical question, *"Who is the god that will deliver you from my hands* (v. 15)?"

The king carried out his threat. "The furnace of fire was heated seven times hotter than it should be heated." The young men were bound, hand and foot, and the slaves of the king cast them into the fire. The fire was so hot that the slaves were themselves burned to death. But alas, when the king looked into the fire he saw not three but four men walking. And the form of the fourth was like the son of God.

Obviously the author of the Book of Daniel was writing a philosophy of history. When people have had to be different, to stand firm in their belief in God, they have indeed had to go through a fiery ordeal. But in that ordeal they have found a god able to deliver them. The world has revolved around heroic souls who have been willing to dare any danger, brave any death, rather than prove disloyal to the highest values they knew.

The story of three Jews is a story with a timeless meaning. Today, in our fast-paced and fragmented world, many people feel lonely and isolated. We have more separation into subdivisions, restricted neighborhoods, private clubs and religious fan clubs than ever before in our history. We have the "academic" community, the "business" community, the "religious" community, the "social" community, the "black" community, the "white" community, the "ethnic" community, the "activist" community and the "professional" community. Some lonely adolescents are so desperate for friends, any friends, that they become involved with drugs just to be a part of the "drug" community.

My friends, we all know that many times we are commanded to bend our knees to certain modes of life not worthy of our allegiance. There's something comforting about huddling together in a community and consolidating a great amount of power. I mean, if we don't all get together we might have to rely on some power greater than our own, and then where would we be? If we don't all join hands and create a community so strong, unified and secure as to defy trouble, who is the god who can deliver us? Nebuchadnezzar's question leaps over the chasm of time and space to demand an answer: "What god can deliver you?"

Jesus made it plain to us. When he knelt in prayer for the last time with his little handful of friends, he made no plea that they be sheltered. He knew they would be stoned, slain with the sword, destitute, afflicted and would wander the deserts and mountains of the earth. There was no cheap and easy way to be a Christian. There still isn't. It takes real character to be a Christian.

If you hear but one theme in this sermon, hear this one: *if you are to be a Christian, you have to possess the courage to be different.* A Christian is not a person with average tastes. A Christian is not a person with average morals. A Christian is not a person with average ideals. A Christian is not a person who bends the knees to the lowest common denominator. Claiming membership in the kingdom of God forever takes you away from the cult of the ordinary. Jesus' question, "Do you really want to be healed?" is no small question. Once you take that name as your name, nothing else matters. It is a serious choice. It makes you different! You become held in the grip of a great moral order which is as firm as granite and as out of step with the values of this earth as a sheep is different from a goat. There is a moral standard in the Bible and you and I are responsible to it. It bridges the chasm between race and race, insisting that we are all eternal neighbors. It bridges the chasm between people who are respectable and those who are outcast. It bridges the chasm between social nobodies and those in lofty places. It makes you a different person. You are called upon to not only love your equals and those beneath you, but to also love those more fortunate than you are, even your enemies. If you are to be a Christian, you have to possess the courage to be different and want the best. The discrepancies amazes me. We faculty want the best pay we can get. We students want in our dormitory rooms and homes the best telephone service we can get, the best food we can buy, the best television we can afford, the best car, and the best job. But we try to get by on average morals. I doubt the President or anyone has to fear that we'll organize and march on Roberts Hall screaming, "We want the best morals we can get." Average is fine in some things. Or is it?

The remaining question, of course, is this: "Where do I get this courage, this moral momentum, to be different?" The apostle Paul hit the nail on the head — "The good I want to do, I don't seem to do. The evil which I want to refrain from doing, I seem to be doing more and more." If being different were easy, we'd all do it all the time and we certainly would not need preachers. Where do we get the momentum to be different?

Basically, we are all creatures of habit. Moral momentum and courage of character come through living right for a series of years. The author of the Book of Daniel kneeled upon his knees three times a day, his windows open toward Jerusalem, and prayed. Jesus Christ went to the synagogue on the Sabbath, even when it was filled with angry people who were threatening his life. The three young men in the story had been following God their whole life and they kept to that habit even though there was an angry king suddenly on the scene. From the habit of doing what you believe to be right, and with each passing year it will become easier to say "no" to each passing temptation. You had to be different to come here today. The majority of Americans do not come to church once a week. The majority of students on a campus don't come to chapel. You were different tonight. Most of them could not say "no" to other diversions. But each time you come, you add a little currency to your habit-forming bank account. You never know when you'll have to draw a little out to pay a bill some day. There's no worse feeling than not having enough spiritual currency inside your soul to pull out in a tempting situation. You can't spend what you don't have. All you can do is bend the knees and fall down like everyone else.

I wasn't around as many notable, socially-oriented people early in life as my wife was in her adolescence. Consequently I never carry enough clothes on a trip. Worse than that, I never carry enough money for things. If you want to find me when you visit Disney World or even Winston-Salem, go to the closest bank that has a 24-hour machine. I'll be in the parking lot.

Shortly after I left graduate school, a former classmate of mine asked me to come to Virginia and perform his wedding ceremony. I really looked forward to it. His father, a physician in Ann Arbor, Michigan, arranged for Diane and me to have a room for four days at a Country Club. We drove into this magnificent estate that had been designed by Thomas Jefferson. Porters in formalwear and white gloves ushered us past the lavish gardens and fountains to a section overlooking the golf course. When the porter opened the door, I thought I'd entered heaven. It was a magnificent suite. "Hmmm," I thought, "I can really get used to this." Now, the porter informed us that the only place around to eat dinner was down in the dining room, and gave us the hours of serving.

At the appointed hour, Diane put on one of the eleven dresses she had brought. I put on the one tie and one sports jacket I'd brought, and off we went to dinner. I was striding rather confidently down the hallway. After all, I'd brought a full $60 in my wallet for the four days. We entered the opulent dining room and were seated at a table while a little man played a violin beside us. I opened the menu, and immediately all the color drained from my face. "My god," I thought. "The decimal points are in the wrong place. Look at these prices."

The maitre'd came up and asked Diane what she would like for dinner. She smiled and pointed to a $22 listing of a steak dinner. I just looked at her and went "Ummmh!" She said, "What's the matter with you?" I responded, "Ummmh!" The waiter then asked for my order. "I'd just like a small salad," I whispered. Diane questioned, "Surely you want more to eat than a salad?" I gave her a non-too-pleasing look and repeated, "No, just a salad."

After a very silent meal, it came time to depart. I asked the waiter for our bill of fare. "Oh," he responded, "your meals are complimentary. The host takes care of them."

Diane knew the system. I didn't. I can't tell you how I felt that night as she walked around with that marvelous steak inside her and that little leafy salad rolled around in my stomach like a B-B inside a bathtub.

Why are we afraid to be different? Basically, I think we just don't know the system. We bend the knees to the cheapest price. When in Rome we do as the Romans do, and when confronted with a decision we do anything for security. The only way to have courage is to trust the host. "Be of courage," said Jesus. "I have paid the bill in full. Great is your reward in heaven. You don't have to feel pressure. It's all right to be different." So be it!

Living Life The Easy Way
Acts 3:1-10
Psalm 118:24

Life is composed of a series of choices and experiences. Usually there is an easy way to accomplish a particular task and there is a hard way to achieve the same end. Many people experience addictions, burnout and nervous breakdowns not because of the sheer weight of their life, but because they fight life. Many people have trouble with college, not because college is hard, but because they fight college. Instead of doing something the best they can, and doing it as easily as they can, they fight the job, fight the experience, fight the assignment, and even fight those around them.

Once, I led a group of friends on an invigorating hike. We had heard that the view from a particular landmark in the mountains was breathtaking. We gathered at the foot of the mountain and began our ascent. For two hours we walked through underbrush, sticker bushes and rotted stumps to get to the top. We saw three snakes and one deer. When we got to the landmark, I was so hungry I didn't know if I still had the energy to stand up. I was sweating profusely from the heat, aching from the scratches and suffering from the bruised knee incurred running from the snakes. When we got to the landmark there was an elderly woman standing there calmly eating an apple and taking pictures. "Good Lord," I thought. "How did that old woman get up here without having a heart attack?"

I asked her, "How on earth did you get here?" She smiled and said, "Oh, I drove up that nice road over there." Then she pointed down the opposite side of the mountain. Sure enough, there was a nice paved road right to the top. We all squeezed into her car and rode back down in 10 minutes. We had fought for two hours to get somewhere we could have driven in 10 minutes.

It happens all the time. I've watched students pay someone to write a paper for them, feverishly copy a fraternity brother's notes from classes they missed, and stay up all night to study for a test. They eked out a "D" for their many hours of labor. All they had to do was come to class three hours a week and read a book for 15 minutes a day. But they chose to fight the experience instead of taking the easy way.

Why do we make life so hard for ourselves? It's a big question. Why do human beings fight life instead of enjoy it? I preach to myself.

Sometimes we fight life because we tell ourselves that's the way life is supposed to be, and we cannot do otherwise. "This runs in the family," becomes our byline. "My grandfather couldn't do it; my father couldn't do it; my brother couldn't do it; I can't do it." Norman Vincent Peale used to say that *"nothing runs in the family except a wrong attitude."*[1] We pass attitudes of limitation on to our children just as people who had a limiting attitude passed it on to us. I have a friend who thinks I helped her with a major problem. She was getting a divorce. She should have gotten a divorce. It was a dying relationship in which she was being thoroughly abused. But her father had a heart attack. She couldn't talk to her father. He wouldn't understand. Besides, they couldn't communicate. He was not a communicative person. Her father hadn't talked to his father. Her grandfather did not know how to communicate with his father. *It ran in the family.*

She knew she would be blown away. The horrible shame of being the only person for three generations to fail at marriage would be an unbearable impediment to any communication, she thought. All I said was, "Nothing has to run in the family."

She timidly drove the long hours to talk with her father. Through the sharing of her pain, her father revealed his unfulfilled ambition to be a math teacher and his pride in having such a successful daughter. She wrote me, "I felt so good after that, I couldn't wait to talk to him again . . . but I never did. He died two months later . . . but I'm grateful I got to know him better."

I imagine some of you visualize her as a timid little person struggling for communication skills who finally learns how to talk. Well, this woman is the anchorperson for a television station in Los Angeles. In one of the largest television markets in the world, she comes into the living room of a million people and communicates with them about life. But it's possible to have all the know-how and smoothness in one aspect of your life and totally fight life in another dimension.

One significant way in which we fight life is to struggle after the wrong dream. At one level we all fight for what has been called the "American Dream." We battle for our particular version of the dream house, the dream family, the dream church, the dream job, the dream life. The most common experience in that battle, of course, is the feeling that we do not have it. Lawrence Reimer notes that the second most common experience is thinking that we are the only person who does not have it. "Everyone else, it seems, is living the American dream, and (we) feel like the American failure."[2] So we try to make our children into something they are not. We try to make our spouse into something he or she is not. We try to make our town, our friends, our job, our church, our values, our roommate and even ourselves into something they are not.

William James, the great psychologist, contended that all the religions in the world appear to meet on two issues. First, that there is an uneasiness about life. There is something wrong about us as we naturally stand. Second, that there is a solution to this uneasiness. The solution is that we are saved from that uneasiness, that wrongness, that difficulty, that hard road by making proper contact with a higher power.[3]

If life were not meant to be uneasy; to be fought against; to be difficult then the pivotal issue is this: what is that solution that enables us to live life the easy way?

The Book of Acts contains the secret. Peter and John were going up to the temple one day. It was in the evening, after the sun had gone down. It was night. On the way, they saw a man with crippled legs sitting by the Beautiful Gate. He was carted there each morning by his parents or friends and put in the same place in order to beg for money. This poor man had to fight life for 40 years.

Along came these happy, healthy men, so the cripple held out his hand, pleading, "Money. Money. Please give me some money."

Peter and John stopped in their tracks and looked at him. Peter finally spoke. "Silver and gold we have none. We haven't any money." Obviously that wasn't very encouraging to the cripple. Peter would have relieved this man's poverty if he could. "But," he said, "we have something else and what we do have, we will give to you." And Peter did all this after first having to get the man to look at them. "Look up at us," he exhorted.

The man had been sitting there with his head down, staring at the dirt. He was a defeated and dejected man. Life had whipped him. Whatever the great dream of life was, he certainly did not have it.

Peter said, "In the name of Jesus Christ, rise up and walk." When the cripple had been lifted up to his feet, he found that he could stand. He took a few steps and he could walk.

What a tremendous story. The man asked for one thing and got something entirely different. He was used to his niche in life; his helplessness ran in the family; he did not have enough money for his dreams. Along came this stranger who said, "Silver and gold have we none. But we do have something else and that something else is what we will give you."

It's a story for the ages. In order to find life, it is that something else that we are truly in need of finding.

There once was a time when God saw the world lying like a cripple at the gates of eternity. This begging world asked only for money and a little comfort to realize its dreams. It ran in the family.

Throughout the family people would come with their temperaments, their sexual drives and their destinies to cry, "Give me a successful venture in this activity, so I can realize my dream." The modern American in a higher, more advanced society would stand, with head down, fighting life, and beg

God, "Money, please. Help me find the solutions to the American dream. I feel like the American cripple. Give me the house, the family, the job, the life of my dreams."

And the great God Almighty, creator of heaven and earth, said, "Look at me. Gaze on me. Look up. Silver and gold I cannot give or guarantee. But I am something else. I have something else. And what I have I will give you. I will give it to you now." To this crippled world, fighting life and living it the hard way, he sent a son, a baby, a man, a spirit to dwell in that world of crippled values and misplaced dreams. He said, "I give you this and it will make you walk and leap and praise me."

Jesus said, "My yoke is easy, not hard. There is an easy way to live life. Follow me and it's yours."

For however long or short a time I am at High Point College you will hear me repeat often what I tell you now. In my career as a minister I have conducted more than 200 funerals. Not once have I heard a single person on their deathbed look back over their life and say, "I wish I had spent more time on my business!" Not one!

To view the college experience or any segment of life only as a time to secure something that will help you acquire silver and gold is a genuine loss. College is not only a time to secure the resources and means by which to earn a living. It is also a time to learn how to live.

Life was meant to be lived in love and service. Life was meant to be lived with God. That's the easy way. There is a flow to life, a pattern of existence. When we surrender to that, instead of fighting it, it's amazing how peaceful and easy life becomes. In spite of lifelong struggles against disease, monetary setbacks, physical and family failures — there is still a way life was meant to be lived. It is amazing how many commonly accepted values in our society actually run against the grain of God's creation.

All who are heavy laden can find an easier way. "Come to me," he says. "Look at me. Get in the flow of my love, my service, my purposes, and you will find your rest."

Life is composed of a series of choices and experiences. There is an easy way and there is a hard way. So be it.

---

1. Norman Vincent Peale, "Why Live Life the Hard Way?" Foundations for Christian Living, 1965, Vol. 16, No. 13, p. 5.

2. Lawrence D. Reimer, *Living at the Edge of Faith* (Valley Forge: Judson Press, 1984), p. 28.

3. William James, *The Varieties of Religious Experience* (Longmans, Green & Co., 1915), p. 508.

Power

2 Corinthians 5:16-17
John 19:19-30

For generations many people have told us that the driving force behind us human beings is the will to power. Power is everything. In fact, God has often been viewed as one who gives power to God's special people. Ancient people prayed for God to give them power over the antelope and the buffalo, whose pictures they drew on the walls of caves. The ancient mariners prayed to Proteus for power over the sea. In our day and time, money is power. So we have prayed for that power and tried to help God along by having power lunches, dressing for success and majoring in business. From age to age the perspective is the same: God is powerful and certainly God can help us get some power, as well.

You learn much about life and power from living in a college dormitory. I've always had a special place in my heart for resident assistants, those students who are paid to help manage a floor in a dormitory. Blessed are the peacemakers. I once served as a dormitory manager in Harvard University. It would have been an easy job except for a student named Dan. Dan was a little scrawny guy with a long red beard. But he made up for his small frame with his over-sized mouth.

Dan's apparent goal in life was to become the world's biggest pest. He was an expert in irritation. When Dan found a chapter he needed to read in a library book, he'd just tear it out of the book, fold it up, stick it in his pocket and walk out of the library with it.

Dan's most annoying trait was late-night use of the pay telephone in our hallway. His girlfriend lived in California. Several nights a week, around 1 a.m., he would pile umpteen quarters and dimes into the phone and converse with her in a loud voice.

Most everyone would pour into the hallway, yelling at me to make Dan get off the phone and give them a chance to sleep. Each time Dan would look up at me and say, quite boldly, "You don't have the power to tell me when to use the phone. Only the telephone company has the power to tell me not to use their phone."

One night while Dan was chattering away with his girlfriend and laying that "You don't have the power" speech on me, Bob walked out of his room. Bob had been an All-American tackle in football at the University of Michigan. He weighed 260 pounds. Without saying a word, Bob ran 10 or 15 feet toward the phone, aimed his shoulder and knocked the phone completely off the wall. Wires whipped everywhere. One of them caught Dan under his armpit, drew blood and knocked him to the floor. Bob looked down at Dan and said, "Now, Dan, *that's power!*"

Believe it or not, at times that's exactly the way some humans have viewed God's use of power. The nation Israel at one point viewed God as a deity who would take all he could stomach of human nature, let Israel's enemies push her almost to the brink, and then knock everything off the wall and start over. At other times God would take all the irritation he could handle from Israel herself. Then he would use another nation to knock Israel off the wall. Power! Certainly power is the ability to forcefully effect a change.

One of the critical issues in the ministry of Jesus Christ was this issue of power. He contended that most of us do not understand the way God uses power. We often ask, "Why does this powerful God allow so much evil in the world?" Why doesn't this God do things differently? While all those Jews and Christians were praying, why didn't God strike down Hitler much sooner?

I would have.

If I had all that power, I would have removed Stalin much earlier. I would have ended slavery much sooner and without a civil war. I would show people how to prevent cancer. If I were all powerful I wouldn't just hear the prayers of people who became rich rather quickly, or scored the winning touchdown.

I would have run Marcos out of the Philippines years before he left and eliminated Kadafy long ago. Now that would be power. Or would it?

Jesus Christ maintained that it takes far less real power to act like that than to use power the way God actually exercises power.

Jesus said, "God is love." God bears our griefs and carries our sorrows: not just at Calvary but all the time. That is certainly a sobering thought. It means that God's power is love and not might. It also means that *God's power is directed toward a purpose: The whole world coming to understand that love is greater than force.* As such, if love is God's goal, God cannot rush to God's end by using the shortest possible means. For example, a teacher could have a great class if he or she simply excluded all the lazy, tiresome and below average students. If you threw out all the non-A students, you'd have a rather exclusive and wonderful class. I've known some teachers, not here, but elsewhere, who use their power in that manner. The very first class they throw out a mile a minute lecture and a reading list that would terrify all but the best students. It just knocks all the below-average students right off the wall. They drop the course and all that's left are good students. It's quite a power play. You can make certain your teaching is evaluated only by good students.

But if your purpose is to reach all students in your class, it's quite another matter. If your purpose is to educate all the students, you can't use power that way.

If God must operate with our world in a similar manner, you and I must ask: Well, then, what power comes to me as a human being when I pray to God? What does prayer do for me? *What power can I claim? Prayer gives us the power of an identity that goes back farther than our own life and extends beyond our death.* It is amazing how human beings can lose their identity. To forget who you are is called amnesia. I'll never forget the time Big Al Geddie forgot who he was.

Big Al was from Mount Olive, North Carolina. He was the biggest athlete recruited in my class at Furman University. Since our colors were purple and white, we had purple helmets with a big white strip down them. That is, everybody but Big Al. Big Al's head was so big he could not wear one of our helmets. The Riddell Company had to make one especially for Al, and it was white. Big Al looked funny out there in his white helmet.

One day, Big Al did not come to class. Then, for a whole week, no one saw him. Nothing in Big Al's room was out of order. His bed was made and his clothes were all there, even his wallet. But no one knew where Big Al was — no one in Greenville knew and no one in Mount Olive, North Carolina, knew. Big Al was lost. Police throughout the South searched for Big Al. Three weeks later Big Al was found. The Atlanta police found him walking around the streets of Atlanta. Big Al didn't know who he was. He had amnesia. Nobody, least of all Big Al who did not know he was Big Al, knew how he got there or where he stayed or how he ate. They took Big Al back to Mount Olive and reintroduced him to his family. They said, "Big Al, meet your momma." And "Big Al, this is your daddy. Big Al, this is where you came from."

Well, after a year, Big Al's memory came back. He remembered who he was and came back to finish college. Big Al didn't forget who he was anymore and eventually graduated.

It must be a horrible thing to forget who you are. Fred Craddock believes that we humans have a residue of our memory of the Garden of Eden. We have a faint reminiscence of a closeness to God. We are all born, created, with this faint memory in our minds. Consequently anyone who cannot attach himself or herself to a memory that stretches back before his or her birth is in real trouble. In essence, prayer gives us the power to tie ourselves to a life that precedes our birth and extends beyond our death. We are enrolled in a story that is beyond our personal story. The roots of who we are lie with the ancient Jews. From them came the Christ. You and I were in Egypt. We were with Abraham. We were in Jerusalem. We saw the star in the east. We were in Antioch. We were at Plymouth, Massachusetts. We were in Valley Forge as the frigid wind blew and the falling snow piled high around our feet. If we do not absorb all that into our awareness, our identity is not complete. We are left orphaned in the 20th century. We are then a victim of amnesia.

Spiritual amnesia can strike anyone. *It is amazing how quickly we human beings can forget we are children of God and should live by love instead of force.* I've forgotten that at times in my life and had to be reintroduced to my heritage.

The president of a bank can forget who he is. The president of a college or dean of a college can forget who he or she really is. Students can come to college and forget who they are. It happens all the time. We get orphaned without memory or our heritage.

I've seen some horrible causes of amnesia. One I'll never forget. A mother raised her child among the rats in a Houston, Texas, ghetto. There were rats coming in and out of the room where they slept and ate. The mother held two jobs — by day she was a teacher's aide; at night she worked in a laundry, folding clothes. With every dollar not needed for the bare necessities, she purchased books for her son. This kid made a perfect score on the SAT — 1600. He went to the University of Texas and made all A's, a 4.0 GPA. Every major graduate school offered him a full scholarship. Yale wanted him. Harvard wanted him. Stanford wanted him. Finally my university sent me and our director of minority recruiting to interview this phenomenon. "Offer him a full scholarship," we were told. "Everybody else has."

We met with him in the lobby of a hotel in Austin, Texas. He began the interview by discounting completely his childhood, dumping on the very environment that had raised him. He let it be known in no uncertain terms that he was going to grab it all. He was going to become a millionaire.

In four years of college life he had not been back to see his mother even once. "I'm beyond that," he said. "We don't have anything in common, intellectually or socially."

We asked him if he'd gone to church or the university chapel or belonged to any service organizations there at UT. "Oh, I'm way beyond that, too," he asserted. "I'm long past that simplistic emotional stuff. That pie-in-the-sky by and by stuff is for poor and unintelligent people."

Rather sadly the recruiter said, "Son, we don't need to offer you a scholarship. We don't want you. Go somewhere else. You don't even know who you are. Your memory is too short if you have one at all. It would be a waste of the school's money to educate you. This suffering, hurting world isn't going to be helped by one more selfish millionaire."

The boy jumped up and angrily spit the words into the face of the recruiter like hot rivets being pounded into a steel girder: "That's okay, one day I'll have the power to bury sentimental saps like you."

I had a strange sense of deja vu. As he walked angrily away from us, in terms of knowing who he was, his amnesia was as great as Big Al Geddie's aimlessly walking the streets of Atlanta. He was paralyzed by a memory that reached back no farther than his own current life.

The disciples went to Jesus one day and asked, "Teach us to pray. It seems to give you a power we don't have." It was one of the few things they ever asked Jesus. And Jesus told them. "When you pray, say, 'Our Father who art in heaven . . .' " or "our parent" and the meaning would be the same. Our father — father of those before our birth and father of those beyond our death. Our father. Our parent. The power of prayer enables us to be placed within a human stream of existence that is eternal. It is identity-forming. It gives us the power to be connected to *an identity that goes back farther than our own life and extends beyond our death.*

Can there be any greater power, any more lasting security? The New Testament clearly crystallizes this new identity of ours. Jesus is called the "angel of the bottomless pit (Revelation 9:11)" — King of all kings; the Lord of all lords. The name that is before and beyond every name. As they moved and breathed, loved and served, Peter and John were asked by the rulers this question: "By what power or by what name do you do this?" In defense, Peter responded, "There is no other name under heaven given among humanity by which we must be saved (Acts 4:7, 12)."

With an identity that began before his own birth and extended beyond his own death, Paul could sweep away every lingering doubt in the believer's mind as to God's power with his series of paired opposites:

neither death	nor life
nor angels	nor powers
nor things present	nor things to come
neither powers from on high	nor powers from below
nor height	nor depth
nor any other creature	

shall ever be able to separate us from the love of God. Now that, my friends, is power!

Real Strength
1 Corinthians 1:25-27
Matthew 5:1-8

In our fast-paced and advertisement-oriented world, it is easy to get trapped. In fact, there are people who specialize in trapping the public.

The invitation comes in the mail. You are invited to visit a new condominium complex at some beach or lake or mountain setting. They'll give you gas money to drive there. They'll give you free lodging and free meals. Why, you even have guaranteed prizes waiting on you, perhaps a new Oldsmobile Cutlass or a color television. Of course, you could also wind up with a cheap transistor radio or a quartz watch instead. All you have to commit to is a 30-minute tour and a short sales pitch. You are free to say "no;" there will be no hard feelings.

How can these companies afford to do this? Well, it's easy. The odds have been figured to the fifth decimal point. Seven and a half percent of visitors will buy because they like what they see. Another 28½ percent will start to give in before they leave. "They've been so good to me! I owe them something. So what if I don't want the property. I shoulda thought of that before I came."[1]

After two or three days of plush living, you can hardly say "no" without feeling like a slob, an ingrate or a rip-off artist. The figures have been researched and they are accurate. In our society, 36 percent of the people will buy something at first sight or give in if they are made to feel like an ingrate or a rip-off artist. It takes real strength to say "no." The figures don't lie. There's a 36 percent chance you and I will give in to anything. That's why major companies now send you magazines or books and simply tell you, "Send it back if you don't want it." No obligation. They know that 36 percent of the people would rather buy something forced on them that they don't really want or need than send it back. In retrospect, I analyzed the figure as I wrote this sermon. Tuesday was registration day at High Point College. This year it was an absolute lock: 36 students, that's all I wanted in each course. True to their word, the courses were closed after 36 students. Bless their hearts, they were tough. The signs were put up: Religion 101A, Closed. Relgion 288, Closed. Religion 109, Closed. But I made the mistake of sitting there at the desk to talk to a few students. Well, after hearing some of the desperate situations, I said "yes" to a few. Now, a 36 percent overload of 36 students would be exactly 49. When I received the rolls the next day, I had allowed exactly 49 students into the courses. I mean, the psychiatrists and the marketing people have got the percentages down to the fifth decimal. *Exactly 36 percent of us will grab at first sight or give in to feelings of being a slob, an ingrate or a rip-off artist. It's so hard to say "no."*

There is a 40 percent chance of divorce in today's world. We cringe at that statistic. But I suspect we are looking at the wrong end of the issue. If the data hold true, then 36 percent of married folk probably never wanted to be married in the first place. They didn't have the strength to say "no." They got trapped. The invitations had been mailed, the caterer was planning to come, and what would the preacher have thought. How could you have returned the gifts? Besides, if you didn't want to marry Susie, you should have thought of that before you did all that other stuff and went this far. It was too late to say "no."

Thirty-six percent of the people co-habitating together outside of marriage probably didn't want to do that in the first place. They got trapped by circumstances. Thirty-six percent of the people who have had sex before marriage probably didn't want to do it in the first place. They got trapped. Thirty-six percent of the people who smoke probably never wanted to smoke in the first place. They got trapped by peer pressure. Thirty-six percent of the people who cheat, commit adultery, or live an amoral lifestyle did not want to do that in the first place. They got trapped by their emotions. People get trapped in jobs they really didn't want in the first place, but someone pays their travel, is nice to them, promises them the moon, and they feel like an ingrate if they say "no." So they move their families and start over somewhere else.

I may be wrong — completely wrong — but I think most of us parents do not fear that our child will grow up to purposefully take drugs, drink too much, join the wrong crowd or be sexually irresponsible. *What we really fear is that our child could become one of the 36 percent of the people who get trapped by life.* If that is true, and there is a 36 percent chance that you and I will give in to anything, then maybe we should view the Bible and its teachings in a new light. The Bible is not a book of rules. It is not a literal history or even a precise compilation of biographies. The Bible is essentially a compilation of people who have interacted with God and found a conscience that helps them understand those experiences and realities in life that are beyond human understanding. *The Bible is a book to help us understand, avoid and move beyond getting trapped by our inability to say "no."*

Dickens said, *"I wear the chains I forged in life."* Is not the pivotal and age-old sin the human belief that we have advanced ourselves to the position where we consider ourselves beyond being trapped? I'm too smart, too experienced, too rich, to fall for that. Is that not the very fabric of the Bible, from Adam and Eve getting trapped by the serpent and the fruit to the righteous, religious folks who were trapped into crucifying Jesus and releasing Barabbas? It takes real strength not to get trapped!

In the realm of personal morality and private morals, we are faced today with some of the saddest demonstrations of decadence in the history of this country. It isn't enough to say "I was trapped," or "we have a nosey press." Morals are such a big issue because we do wear the chains we forge in life. Jesus is right: "He who is unfaithful with little will be unfaithful with much." If there is sexual freedom before marriage, and people violate their principles before marriage, it's hard to avoid trouble after marriage. The person who cheats before he or she attains a responsible position in the company will face many more temptations to cheat after a responsible position has been reached. The farther you travel in life the more opportunities, not fewer, you have for wrongdoing. You think it's easy to lose your moral fibre at 18? Wait until you're 38 or 48 or 58.

How does a person find real strength in life? How do we keep from getting trapped, from leaping at the first thing we see or from feeling like an ingrate, a slob, or a rip-off artist if we say "no?" Essentially, whether we practice them or not, I think we all come to realize the truth in Jesus' teachings. We do live in a moral universe. None of us is free. A mother went into pain and labor so that we could be here. We all carry the name of our father. A Savior hung on a cross, bleeding to death, like a slab of meat, for six to ten hours so we could gather here with some knowledge of a forgiving and loving God. Born free? None of us is born free. This same Savior promised that if we would learn afresh each day what God wanted for us, his mind could be in us to keep us from getting trapped. He also articulated some strange ideas about real strength and real happiness in life. Happy and strong are the pure in heart. Happy and strong are they that mourn and cry. Happy and strong are the meek, not the smart-alecks or wiseguys. Happy and strong are the peacemakers. Happy and strong are those people who go two miles when asked to go one. Happy and strong are those who do not commit adultery but keep themselves under control. Happy and strong are the people who not only love their friends but also love and pray for their enemies. Such people do not leap at everything. Nor do they feel guilty or unpopular when they say "no" to something or someone. They realize that ultimately we all have to live longest with ourselves. It's the sure shots, not the hot shots who really make it.

Major League baseball Commissioner Peter V. Ueberroth was asked to speak about the finest and strongest athlete he had ever seen. Ueberroth should be a good person to comment on athletics and strength. He directed the Olympic Games in Los Angeles. He saw Carl Lewis, the wrestlers, the weightlifters, all of them. As commissioner of baseball, he worked with all three major television networks. He has seen Jose Canseco, Roger Clemens, Dwight Gooden, Mark McGruire, Mickey Mantle, Willie Mays, Dave Winfield, Hank Aaron — all of them. He ought to know real strength if anyone does.

Peter Ueberroth stood in Kenan Stadium in Chapel Hill, North Carolina, and gave his answer to thousands of people. The finest and strongest athlete he ever saw was quite clear. He encountered this athlete a month before the Olympic Games. The Olympic torch was being run across America by relay. Every runner, in order to run, had to donate $3,000 to a charity in his or her hometown. That's how you got to run. Donate $3,000 and you could run the torch a kilometer, about six-tenths of a mile, and pass it to someone else who had also donated $3,000. People would stand five or six deep along the roadside to watch and cheer these runners.

At one point in the relay, a female runner finished her run with the torch with a strong stride. When her kilometer was up, she bent over to light the torch of the next runner.

And this next runner had to hold the torch with two hands. She was a little nine-year-old girl. Everyone could see that she was severely crippled. Obviously, she could not run a kilometer. But they lit her torch anyway. There was a policeman there with a big white plastic helmet on, gunning his motorcycle engine impatiently. He started ahead, waiting for her to take a step. She tried to take one halting step after another. Finally, she was able to limp with a little cadence, going hesitating step after hesitating step.

She had trained for a year with a 10-pound hammer because the torch weighed nine pounds — but it was still obvious that she wasn't going to make a kilometer.

Everyone learned later that the little crippled girl and her mother raised the $3,000 by bake sales and garage sales to donate to charity in her little town in New Mexico.

This little girl had a huge smile on her face as she limped along. She kept going, with the huge torch wobbling in her two hands. She became wringing wet with perspiration and slowed almost to a stop several times. As she walked, a strange thing happened. Instead of being five deep along the roadside, the crowd became 10 deep and 20 deep and 30 deep. They had banners saying, "Run Amy Run. Run Amy Run." And people started to cheer. Her whole school turned out. She was exhausted, but this beautiful smile was still on her face. The little athlete made her kilometer. She lit the flame of the next runner who was off like a shot. There was a special look of triumph on her face as she stood there. She had achieved something very, very special. And on the side of the road was a motorcycle policeman. He had his plastic helmet up and a huge white handkerchief wiping his eyes.

Peter Ueberroth states flatly: *"This young lady . . . was the finest and strongest athlete that I ever saw."*[2]

It takes real strength not to get trapped by your body, weak or strong. It takes real strength not to get trapped by your anger or your emotions. It takes real strength to deny yourself in order to contribute to others. It takes real strength to go out in public when all might laugh at you. It takes real strength to labor over and over again to reach a mighty and lofty goal. It takes real strength to triumph over life and not become trapped by it.

In our diverse and fast-paced world, you and I do not need different circumstances. We need real strength. And that's exactly what Jesus tried to tell us.

So be it.

---

1. Data furnished in Art Greer, *The Sacred Cows Are Dying* (New York: Hawthorn, 1978).

2. Peter V. Ueberroth told the story in his commencement speech at The University of North Carolina, May 10, 1987, Chapel Hill, North Carolina.

Belief And Behavior

Compassion
The Cracking Point
The Necessity Of Forgiveness
The Housing Problem
The World's Best Kept Secret

Compassion
Luke 10:25-37

One of the pivotal questions in life is this one: *"What does it mean to grow up?"* How do you know when someone is mature? When is someone real?

Most of the time it doesn't have anything to do with age. I've known some 20-year-old girls who live like they're 75-year-old old maids. And occasionally friends will even ask me what I'm going to do when I grow up.

What does it mean to grow old? When buying a ticket to a movie theatre, you're an adult when you reach 13 years of age. The state says you're old enough to drive when you are (depending on your state law) 15 or 16. They say you're old enough to drink alcoholic beverages when you're 21 and to vote when you're 18.

Margery Williams gave a classic answer in a book, *The Velveteen Rabbit*. It is the story of a little boy's nursery. The nursery was full of toy animals. One day a new toy rabbit came to live there. The rabbit wanted to know the secret of becoming real. He asked the skin horse, who was so old his brown coat was rubbing off, how to become real.

The old horse responded, "Real isn't how you're made, Rabbit. It's a thing that happens to you. When a child loves you for a long, long time . . . then you become real." The rabbit then asked, "Does it hurt?"

"Sometimes," he answered. "Generally by the time you are real, most of your hair has been loved off, and your eyes drop out and you get loose in the joints and are very shabby. But these things don't matter at all because once you are real you can't be ugly, except to people who don't understand."

Real isn't how you're made. Real isn't how old you are. It is a thing that happens to you. And the skin horse was right. It can be wearing to be loved by someone.

The most important thing in the world is to become "real." What matters is loving and being loved for a long, long time. Loving and being loved add wrinkles and white hairs to your head and can make joints grow loose.

I have always been fascinated by the attempts of various societies and cultures to conjecture what Jesus Christ must have looked like. If he was real, what did he look like? In the 1950s, most of the pictures of Christ available to us were somewhat effeminate. We've encountered scores of paintings depicting a Jesus with long brown hair, baby smooth skin and a glowing halo around his head. He looked like a very thin, pious 33-year-old wimpish Peewee Herman with manicured fingernails. Then, in the 1960s, largely due to preachers' attempts to break out of being perceived as a kind of third sex, we had an emphasis on Jesus as a real man's man. The rugged carpenter came into focus. The man who could do all that walking and speaking must have had real stamina. Consequently, we perceived Jesus as a tough Mel Gibson or Sylvester Stallone look-alike with muscles flexed and a jogger's pair of legs. Then, in the 1970s, we tried to reconcile Jesus' appearance with the fantastic sums of money pouring into the coffers of televisions evangelists. "Jesus only deserves the very best," became our watchword. As Pat Robertson explained to visitors to his 700 Club headquarters in Virginia Beach, when they asked about the expensive paneling flown in from England or the opulent antiques decorating even more opulent rooms, "We think Jesus, when he returns to earth, is going to return here first, and we want him to have the very best." So we encountered a Jesus who resembled Prince Charles or Donald Trump, a kingly, regal man with a white cloud for transportation.

Personally, if Jesus was as much human as divine, like the Bible says he was, I think none of those depictions are accurate. Jesus was not only a Messiah and a Risen Lord. Jesus was a wonderful, compassionate person. He was a real person. He loved and was loved for a long time, and showered his compassion on everyone he met. Perhaps the truest statement is that of Peter: "Jesus went about doing good (Acts 10:38)."

Jesus loved, and then when you do good you sometimes get hurt. Have you ever seen the hurt in a child when it trusts someone and that trust is betrayed? Have you ever seen a woman whose husband abuses her, abandons her, takes her money and leaves her for another person? It takes psychiatrists, friends and hospitals a few years to try to correct some of that damage and convince her that being a good person really isn't that bad a lifestyle. Have you ever seen what happens to a man whose best friends abandon him in an hour of need and then try to throw him to the wolves? Think about these things and read the life of Jesus between Christmas and Easter. Christianity must never leap from the songs and bells and candles and presents of Christmas to the flowers and Handel's *Messiah* of Easter without passing by the dusty roads of Galilee and Judea, places where Jesus was showing compassion. Think of it. He heals 10 lepers and one returns to thank him. If that were me, I'd make the other nine sick again. But he doesn't. He bears it. He asks his friends to stay up with him while he goes off to a garden and, in great anxiety and depression, sweats big drops of sweat so big, one writer says they flowed like blood. Then he comes out and witnesses those friends sound asleep. "Could you not stay awake one hour?" he asks. I know how it feels when a student sleeps 50 minutes. All of Jesus' students fell asleep. Finally, one of the 12 best friends he has on earth sells him out to his enemies for a little pouch of money.

My guess is that the man who walked to Calvary was prematurely gray. He must have seemed more like 63 than 33 years old in appearance. His face must have contained more wrinkles than mine and his joints must have been quite loose. He probably was dead broke and mentally worn by all the sacrifices he had made. But he was the most real person who ever lived. He had more compassion than all of us put together. He was the most beautiful person who ever lived. He was ugly only to those people who didn't understand.

For me, the time between Christmas and Easter symbolizes the most critical time in the life of the Christian. This is the time that affords us an opportunity to become real.

Real is not how we are made. It is a thing that happens to us. The gold, frankincense and myrrh have been put away in the storage rooms above the organ chambers. The Easter flowers have not yet been ordered. We are in the gaps between Christian festivals. But, my friends, *it is in life's gaps that we become real.* Jesus told us a parable about how people become real. Real is not how you are made. It is something that happens to you. Jesus said a man was beaten and left half-dead. He was unconscious and his clothes were torn off. He was simply "a certain man." There was no clue whatsoever as to his status or his accent. All we know is that he was in need. A priest came by and would not get near him. In those days one had to handle a dead body in a special way; otherwise you were defiled. A life was hanging in the balance, but the priest was worried about staying pure and not getting defiled by an improper involvement.

Then a Levite came by also. Ah, a Levite. Upper-middle class. The best education money can buy. It was not his stature to get involved with people beneath his status or proper family. Since the man had no clothes or speech, who could tell what rank he came from? He couldn't take a chance on being seen on the Jericho road associating with just anybody. The rumors would ruin him.

Then a Samaritan came by. Jesus said, "The Samaritan was filled with compassion." He was not concerned with the man's pedigree, his race, or the cause of his tragedy. He simply had compassion. Compassion. Jesus said, "You go and do the same." Have compassion. The person may never be capable of returning the favor, but you go and have compassion. The ten may not thank you; your friends may abandon you; your buddies may sell you out, but you go and have compassion.

It is a charge that causes us to shiver. Deep down, I think most of us know that in spite of our achievements in technology and medicine, our society is no better off morally and spiritually than those people who heard the original version of this story so long ago. We still haven't found a way to educate people in compassion. We grant more degrees than the world has ever seen before. We also have more casual but painful divorces, more child abuse, more wife and husband abuse, more suicides, more homeless people sleeping in garbage cans, more people destroying themselves through death-dealing drugs, more people treating children as if they asked to be born in poor neighborhoods, and more penalties for indigent adults who grow old and get sick. *You and I need to recover a sense of human compassion if any society ever did.* And "real" is not how you are made; it is something which happens to you. That is indeed the hope of the world — that enough people can become "real" to enable this earth to be a better place for those who come after them. You can become a good business person without becoming "real." You can become a good lawyer without becoming "real." You can have children and not be real. You can become a minister and not be real. Compassion cannot be bought. You can't purchase it.

The world relies on compassionate people to train us as to the values of life. Several months ago, I received a phone call from a friend of mine from a distant state. This lady and her husband were very well-off financially. In fact, their combined incomes exceed $10 million a year. They are worried about their 21-year-old son. His marriage only lasted six months. He has no job. He just lives in a condominium by himself. He is on drugs. He got in over his head and washed out of college. His parents never know where he is or who his friends are. So his mother had conjectured a possible scenario. "Hal," she said, "Do you think I could find a 'Mr. Perfect' somewhere and hire him to go live with my son, show him the ropes, let him go to college with him, and help him plan out some choices in life?" The thought shocked me. "Hal," she continued, "you've got your life together. Who was your mentor? Can't I hire someone to do for him what someone obviously did for you?"

I responded in rather direct fashion. "There are no perfect people, for starters. Secondly, my life is not all that together. Everyone has problems. But most important, you cannot go out and buy 40 years of compassion."

I thought of the aunt who took off from work in Charlotte to stay with me for a week while my sister was born; the high school principal who kept me in school and gave me a job when I was running around with the wrong crowd and deserved to flunk out; the college coach who made Furman admit me when I did not deserve to be admitted and had a projected GPA of 1.8; the minister who gave me a job when I had no experience; the college cheerleader who copied an extra set of notes from our English and history classes for three weeks while I was in Greenville General Hospital having knee surgery. I thought about the family in South Carolina, whose names I did not know and the university will never give me, who paid my entire tuition bills my last two years at Harvard; the doctors who hired my wife for a full-time job over the telephone 1,000 miles away even though they had never met her; she did not have one day's experience in the field, and she spoke Southern instead of Yankee; the 350 people in my first church who smiled, affirmed and loved me for two years even though I did not know how to preach; the 11 people from High Point who drove 500 miles roundtrip to attend a 20-minute funeral for my father.

Now, how and where would you tell someone they could hire that? Finally, I told my friend — "Actually, I have never had my life very much together. I've just been the recipient of more compassion than most people. There isn't enough money in the world to buy the compassion I have received. There is only one thing you can do. You can start showing your son and everyone around you some compassion, even though they may not seem to deserve it. Most likely they will not thank you. Read the parable of the Good Samaritan."

The world will still have its problems. You can't solve the problems of the world. You can't feed every hungry child in Africa. You can't solve the problems of drug abuse and divorce. You can't solve the civil rights problem or the problems of women's rights. But God can take you and focus you on something. You can at least become real.

Real isn't how you are made. It is something that happens to you. "A certain man fell into trouble and a certain Samaritan, when he saw the man, was filled with compassion. You go then, and do the same."

The Cracking Point
Mark 12:1-12

Everyone has a cracking point. There comes a certain point in our relationships with others or in our feelings about ourselves when everything snaps. You and I are emotionally and physiologically structured so that we can withstand only so much. There is only so much garbage, so much heat we can take. Then, like the valve on a pressure cooker, we simply blow off. Perhaps the six most dramatic words in the English language are these: "I just can't take it anymore."

Every person has a cracking point. It happens to even the most passive and sedate person. I'll never forget an incident from my childhood. It occurred when I was 13 years old. My best friend's family used to gather on certain weekends in the fall at their "old homeplace" near Atlanta. They frequently included me on their trips.

We would all go to a college football game in Atlanta on Saturday. Then on Sunday after lunch all the aunts, uncles, brothers, sisters and assorted friends like me would bid one another farewell. My friend's father, Mr. W., was one of the nicest, most even-tempered persons I have ever met. He was always in command of his emotions.

One Sunday, as we packed the car to return home, it started raining. All the relatives were gathered on the porch watching Mr. W. pack the trunk. His wife came out in the yard and stood there under her umbrella giving Mr. W. instructions. For 10 minutes or more she kept up an incessant cadence of instructions. "Put this here; put that there." Finally, Mr. W. had had enough. He started flinging items out of the trunk and all over the yard. Mr. W. flung all the suitcases, garment bags, travel kits and everything. Clothes were everywhere: in the mud and on the hedges. Mrs. W. just stood there crying in the rain. I can still visualize her holding that umbrella and crying while all the relatives on the porch were laughing. One of them whispered in my ear, "Mr. W. just hit his cracking point."

Those points exist for everyone. A problem begins in loneliness, fear, anger, busted relationships, lack of communication, resentment or stress and we reach a cracking point. Then the debris from that moment is scattered all over the backyard of our horizon. Sometimes we, unlike Mr. W., don't have a lot of relatives and friends to come running off the back porch and start repacking life for us. Sometimes all we can do is stand in the rain and scream, "I just can't take it any more."

In a recent survey the American Medical Association asked several thousand general practitioners across the country, "What percentage of people that you see in a week have needs that you are qualified to treat with your medical skills?" The responses ranged from one percent to 25 percent. The average was 10 percent. In other words, 90 percent of the people who see a general practitioner have no medically treatable problem. Most of the respondents said they prescribed tranquilizers. The patients are ill and suffering real pain. They may even die prematurely. But essentially a problem that begins when lifestyles and relationships reach a cracking point moves from one bodily system to another until it stops at some particular organ with nowhere else to go. Then it becomes defective and the doctor can practice "end organ medicine."[1]

Everybody has a cracking point. And God can identify with that. God has a "cracking point," too. There have been times, if Scripture is correct, when God has reached his cracking point. That point for God seems to come when humans attempt to forget they are tenants of this world and not owners.

It started with Adam and Eve. The Lord gave them everything. He put up with everything they did except one thing. The hunger of man he put up with and even built a garden. The loneliness of man beat him down so he built a companion. The dominance of humans gnawed at him so he let the humans name every living thing on the planet and have dominion over them. All he said was "I don't want you to try to take over and become like me. Enjoy what I've given, but I couldn't take your trying to take over the knowledge of good and evil."

But an evil force came along and said, "God won't crack. Don't worry about it. You can do anything. You can have your eyes opened and be like God."

So they tried it. And that was God's cracking point. At the time of their greatest success, Adam and Eve ran into God's cracking point. Like a madman hurling baggage from the trunk of a car, God called out the debris he was going to leave all over the backyard of humankind. "I will greatly multiply your pain in childbirth; you will have to earn a living all the rest of the days of your life; you will sweat and toil; and when that's over, you will return to the ground from which you were taken; you are dust and to dust you shall return (Genesis 3:16-19)." Then God drove them out of the garden.

In reality, the response from God seems all out of proportion to the mistake — from our point of view. But not to God. Arrogance is his cracking point.

As we view the Bible, we can say God's cracking point is consistent, from the Tower of Babel, when humans tried to reach into the heavens and God busted them into different languages, to his relationship with the Pharaoh. When Pharaoh tried to own something that wasn't his and God cut down the innocent children, the cracking point came when humans tried to be like God and take over.

The last parable Jesus ever told points to God's cracking point (Mark 12:1-12). After Jesus told this parable, his enemies finally ganged up on him. The record states, "The scribes and chief priests tried to lay hands on him at that very hour." All the top level Jewish brass were in agreement. This prophet from Nazareth had to be silenced forever.

The parable of the wicked tenants pictures a God dealing with humans who resent the fact that they are only humans. They want to be God. A man plants a vineyard, digs a pit for a winepress, rents it out to tenants and leaves. When harvest time arrives, this owner sends a servant to get some fruit from the tenants. They beat him up and run him off. Twice more the owner sends servants. They beat one of them up and kill the other one. All the owner has left is a beloved son. So he sends him, saying, "They will respect my son." But the renters have become profiteers. They want to steal the property.

Under Jewish law, three years undisputed possession of a piece of land enabled a person to claim ownership of that land over the holder of a deed. The tenants were elated when the son came. They got their hands on the heir. So they killed the owner's son.

Jesus reported, "What will the owner do? He will come and destroy the tenants."

When the scribes and priests heard this, they exclaimed, "God forbid!"

Now, my friends, immediately following this parable, Jesus was asked, "Is it lawful to pay taxes to Caesar or not?" Jesus simply responded, "Give Caesar the things that Caesar owns and give God the things God owns."

Obviously, the meaning is clear — *woe, be unto us if we try to give ourselves the things that God owns.* That's God's cracking point.

Now the central matter is this. Most of our problems in life come when we turn over to ourselves things that don't belong to us. When we try to play God, we crack up. When we use other creatures to selfishly maintain our own high standard of living, we crack up. When our own ambition wildly leads us to covet things that are not ours, we crack up. When we sever relationships with other people and jealously try to steal for ourselves the integrity of those other people, we crack up.

But humans and God have in common more than the ability to reach the cracking point and shout into the rain. "I just can't take it any more." We and God still live on after our cracking points. There's life beyond the cracking point. In fact what we do with life beyond the cracking point is more important than what happens up to that moment. People do live beyond their cracking point. And we can look to God for an example of how to do that, as well. *When you get on the other side of your cracking up point, that's when you have to return to your essential faith in a God of love.* That's when you have to get down to basics.

One spring day in Washington, D.C., an excursion boat was on the Potomac on its maiden run. A large number of Congressmen and Senators were invited. The day was a hot one. So a famous Senator removed his shoes and socks. He hung the socks on a railing in front of him. One of the members of the press noticed that someone ran by him and inadvertantly brushed against one of the socks. It fell into the water and was gone. The Senator went over to the railing, picked up the remaining sock and threw it overboard. The columnist was impressed. He confessed that if it had been him he probably would have brought the remaining sock home. "I have a . . . drawer full of single socks . . ." he said. "That's my problem. My life is full of single socks. I've got to clean out these good for nothing things and get down to some new simple basics that work."[2]

Sometimes after our cracking points you and I carry around things we should throw away about ourselves and God. Things and beliefs sometimes get lost and need to be jettisoned so we can return to a new appreciation of what God did after he reached his cracking point. There is a tendency for us to go through life mesmerized by our past losses and hurts. We tend to forget what God has done for us. Instead of a firm belief in a loving God, we hold on to a drawer full of religious single socks. We forget that what God did in Jesus after his cracking point was the match to what he did to Adam and Even and the wicked tenants in the vineyard. *The New Testament account of the cross is the matching sock to everything we fear about God.*

Perhaps the best dramatization of God's cracking point and afterwards was given by a man from Greensboro named Marc Connelly. In 1929, Connelly, a black man, wrote a play called *The Green Pastures.*[3] It was an attempt to portray in the language of uneducated blacks from the deep South, a vision of God and his heaven. The play opened in New York in February of 1930 and ran for over a year and a half. In Connelly's view of heaven the angels hold some magnificent fish fries. The final scene revolves around just such a fish fry. A large kettle of hot fat has a fire going underneath it. A rustic table is piled high with piles of biscuits and cornbread, and the cooked fish are in huge dish pans. There are two large churns of custard which looks like milk. There are glasses and a dipper beside the churns. The angels are milling around, flapping their wings. But God is seated in an armchair with his face in his hands. Every now and then he looks up and stares out toward earth and cries. The angel Gabriel walks in and comes up to the armchair.[4] "You look worried, Lawd."

God nods his head.

"Here, have a cigar, Lawd."

But God says, "No thanks, Gabriel; don't want no cigar."

Gabriel goes over and gets a cup of custard. Then he returns. "You look awful, Lawd. You look awful. You been sittin' yere, lookin' dis way, an awful long time. Is it somethin' serious, Lawd?"

God responds: "Very serious, Gabriel. Look at my chillun down there on earth. They's killing one another. Stealin' from and lying' to each other. They's committin' adultery and runnin' after money. My heart's broken."

Gabriel is awed by his tone. He knows the Lord just can't take it any more. "Lawd, is de time come for me to blow de horn? Just say the word, Lawd. Just snap you finger and I'll blow de horn. We'll wipe 'em all out dead right now. Worse than Adam. Worse than Noah. Worse than Pharaoh. Say de word, Lawd, and I'll blow de horn."

God waves Gabriel off. "Not yet, Gabriel; I've decided what I'm gonna do. Ain't but one thing left to do. I'm a gonna go down there myself. I'm gonna live among 'em. Eat among 'em. Love 'em. Help 'em. Even die among 'em if I have to."

The Lawd gets up from his armchair and walks away from the fish fry. Gabriel goes over to the empty chair and he stares down at earth. All the heavenly beings come over and look down, too. And from the back a voice is heard: "Oh look at him! Look at him. Dey goin' to make him carry that cross up dat high hill! Dey goin' to nail him to it! Dey goin' to nail him to it! Oh dat's a terrible burden . . ." But as the light fades, they see the Lawd down there smiling gently. And all the angels burst into song. Cause they'd seen what the Lawd had done after he got to his cracking point.

---

1. See Bruce Larson, *There's A Lot More To Health Than Not Being Sick* (Waco, Texas: Word, Inc., 1981), p. 20.

2. *Ibid*, p. 132.

3. *The Green Pastures* was first produced at the Mansfield Theatre, New York City, by Laurence Rivers, Inc., on February 26, 1930 and closed on August 29, 1931. Marc Connelly's original play may be found in *Sixteen Famous American Plays,* edited by Bennet Cerf and Van H. Cartwell (Garden City, New York: Garden City Publishing Co., 1941). It was produced in many versions. I have used a combination of the original and later productions, trying to retain the meaning and purpose of the original while fitting some of the language into my sermon.

4. *Ibid*

The Necessity Of Forgiveness
Luke 7:36-50

I speak to you tonight about forgiveness. We all need to forgive more. *People who do not learn how to forgive do not enjoy life.* The world hands us many irritating people. Some of them frustrate us to no end. If we embrace resentment instead of forgiveness, our relationships and our careers don't get very far. If you want to be a success in the world — major in forgiveness.

A newspaper carried the story of a man who bought a new Cadillac. Every time the car hit a slight bump there was an awful thumping. Twice he took the car to be examined. But they never could find the cause. Always there was the thumping. Finally, the servicemen narrowed the problem to one door of the car. When they took the door apart, they found a coke bottle inside. In the bottle was a note which read: "So you finally found me, you wealthy _____ _____ _____ _____ (blankety-blank)." You see, a worker was so filled with resentment he thought he could destroy the satisfaction of the person who had enough money to buy a Cadillac. Actually, the worker's grudges and resentments had infested his own mind and his everyday job. The satisfaction being destroyed was his own.[1] Thus he made his work-life a slave to his perceived enemies.

Our greatest danger in resentment lies not in the wrong done to us but in the wrong we can do to ourselves if we let ourselves become inwardly hardened. Can you imagine having to work in a job which stirs up a vindictive response in you? Who has the reward? You or your enemy?

How impossible Jesus' ideal seems at first — "love your enemies and pray for them that persecute you." But it is not impossible. In fact, on second glance it seems to be the most practical and rational rule for daily living that could be laid down. The only rewards in life come through working through relationships. There is no reward in having a small circle of like-minded friends.

Doris Donnelly in her incisive book, *Learning to Forgive*,[2] tells about a family she knew. They were very proficient in the use of resentment. They couldn't forgive anyone, nothing was ever their fault. The family consisted of two parents and their three daughters. The friends of each family member were under constant scrutiny to determine whether or not they belonged to their group. The family socialized together, sat together in church, and participated in the community, all as a small group. Failing to include the three sisters in a birthday celebration, or not greeting a member of the group with beaming smiles and deferential courtesy, resulted in ostracism. The family lived to be stroked by others. One year the parents gave the same Christmas gift to each of the daughters' teachers, to the pastor of the church and to the principal of the school. Anyone who did not respond immediately with profuse gratitude was eliminated from the list for the next time. The family took every delay as a personal slap in the face. And everyone scissored out of their lives knew there was little hope of being sewn into their lives again.

The mother of the family died suddenly. The father and the daughters naturally expected large crowds to gather for the final farewells. They enlisted the aid of the local police to handle traffic on the morning of the funeral. Phone calls were made to neighbors and to their "friends." Announcements were sent via telegram to people who had moved away. The local motels were alerted to save a few rooms for out-of-town guests who might appear at the last minute and need accommodations. Exactly 10 people showed up for the funeral. The husband, the daughters, their husbands, one grandchild and two members of their small circle of friends attended the services. It was truly embarrassing. The town laughed about it for years afterward.

People who scissor others from relationships think they are cutting people out of their lives. In reality they are cutting themselves out of the larger human family. They not only die alone, but whether they know it or not, they live alone as well.

It is a fact of existence that small circles of mutual resentments are not easily broken. You can take a group of goldfish that have been swimming for their lifetime in a small fish bowl out to the lake. You can turn them loose in the lake, but they will continue to swim in small circles, the dimension of their former bowl, for quite a while without accepting the massive freedom awaiting them. Jesus called the phenomenon "saluting only your brethren." And he told it straight — "what reward is there in that?" It creates an attitude of smallness which is destructive to career, family and self.

During the ministry in the villages of Galilee, Jesus preached passionately about forgiveness. It was a strange doctrine to most of the disciples. Peter wanted to be legal and statistical about it. But Jesus stated there is no limit to forgiveness. It's a matter of forgiveness becoming a part of the habit of your life. You can't forgive people 490 times without it becoming a permanent attitude. You cannot serve two masters. Either you will bow before the altar of revenge and scissor people out of your life; or you will bow before the altar of forgiveness and sew yourself to the wider fabric of humanity, as imperfect and impulsive as it is.

Peter had not realized the greatness of forgiveness. You cannot forgive someone and pray for them, even if they persecute you, without becoming a person of love. Forgiveness creates a loving spirit. Jesus told Peter, "You must forgive from your heart." The key word is *kardia* which is translated "heart." But the Greek word means more than the organ of the body. It means the seat of the inner person. Forgiveness is more than an act we do; it is an expression of who we are.

Look at how it worked in the lives of those around Jesus. In the example of the woman who received forgiveness from Jesus, the main object of the teaching is Simon Peter (Luke 7:36-50). Simon Peter was not a loving person to begin with. Jesus contrasts the conduct of the woman with that of Simon.

The woman was loving and kind. She loved Jesus very much. And she had many sins to be forgiven for. But her actions, her deeds, indicated that she had become a new person. Simon was, of course, quite satisfied with his righteousness. He had experienced no forgiveness which might have made real for him the personal mercy of God. In his personal relationship with people, then, he exhibited little or no love. Simon didn't even extend the little customary courtesies to Jesus when he entered Simon's house. So Jesus blatantly stated, "The person who is forgiven little, who is self-righteous and proud, scissoring out those who are less righteous, loves little."

Apparently, though, Jesus' life of forgiveness wore off on Peter. Perhaps it was Jesus' forgiveness in Peter's presence of the soldier who came to arrest Jesus and experienced Peter's cutting his ear off. Perhaps it was the frightful experience of hearing those words of forgiveness uttered by Jesus toward his enemies as he painfully died on the cross. Whatever precipitated it, Peter apparently grasped the greatness of forgiveness. Following Christ's death, Peter wrote a letter to Christians in the northern part of Asia Minor. We know it as the Book of First Peter. Peter began the second chapter with these words: ". . . strip away all malice and all guile and insincerity and envy and all slander . . . for you have tasted the kindness of the Lord (1 Peter 2:1, 3)."

What an incredible power forgiveness turns loose. It is an expansive spirit. A person who has done his or her best and seen others walk off with what he wanted, who has planned and missed, aspired and failed, but can still walk through life with an unenvious and forgiving heart, being happy in his own best self, is a person who has won a great victory. That person is a slave to no one. Life itself becomes his or her ally instead of enemy.

The central thesis in Jesus' assertion about the kingdom of God was that small circles of people would become increasingly larger circles of people through winning over and including their perceived enemies. That is the acid test of Christianity. *Virtually every other group in society can do everything else Christians can do.*

Christians have programs. So does every other group. Christians recite creeds — so do sororities, fraternities and 1,000 other groups. Christians sing songs. So does every group, from "99 bottles of beer on the wall" to *The National Anthem.* Christians raise money. So does everyone else.

Frankly, friends, we are revealed only by the way we forgive other people, especially our enemies.

The greatness of Christianity lies not in its development of small pockets of congenial intimacies. The greatness of Christianity is in its expansive spirit that overthrows resentments, takes in enemies, embraces rivals and seeks the good in all sorts of people across all barriers that class and race can erect.

Everyone in this room belongs to a group — whether the Board of Stewards, a sorority, a faculty, a church, a club, a class. What can your group do that other groups can't do? What can you as an individual do that really makes you stand out and feel good about yourself. The answer is simple — forgiveness.

---

1. See *His Hands: Resources for Lent and Easter,* ed. Jon L. Joyce (Lima, Ohio: C.S.S. Publishing Co., 1977), p. 64.

2. Doris Donnelly, *Learning to Forgive* (New York: Macmillan, 1979), pp. 24-25.

The Housing Problem
Luke 11:17-36
1 Timothy 5:3-6

One of the most nerve-wracking experiences in life is finding a place to live. It's as true for college students as it is for older adults. Everyone at some time or another has to house-hunt, roommate hunt, room hunt or apartment hunt. In fact, one of the biggest changes in life occurs at the end of the freshman year in college when you can actually have a choice as to where you will live and with whom you will live.

The freshman experience is an unknown experience. The school assigns you a roommate and a place to live. You have little choice in the matter. It can produce some rather odd roommates. I remember my freshman year. I was assigned to room with a student from Florida. He rolled up the tube of toothpaste; I liked to squeeze the toothpaste. My idea of a fun Friday night was a fraternity party or a ball game; for him it was going to the library to read the back issues of the Jacksonville newspaper. He thought our closet was where you organized your clothes; I thought it was where you threw things you didn't want people to see. It was a happy day for both of us when we could change.

House-hunting is important. Come spring you'll witness students camping out at the AC's office to sign up for a place to live. And no housing is perfect. Those who want to live with their sisters in Millis have to have a community bath. But they'll tell you it's worth the sacrifice. Those who want a frat house have no washers and driers nor air-conditioning, but they'll tell you it's worth it. If you want to live in Belk you share a suite with athletes. Then there are the neighbors to deal with.

In that regard we're all alike. *Until the day we die we have to deal with neighbors.* Many people my age still ask: "How can people be so selfish, so cruel, so indifferent to others?"

And we still have trade-offs. Large house and privacy? The more taxes and utilities you have to pay. The better the bargain, the more upkeep on the house. In short, there'll always be a housing problem.

One of the clear claims of the New Testament is that the devil also goes house-hunting. In a rather direct way, the spirit of evil starts poking around our neighborhoods looking at your household and mine, seeing if it might be ripe for take over. It makes sense. *If there's evil in the world, it's got to live somewhere.* Jesus actually told a parable about the devil going house-hunting. An unclean spirit was thrown out of a house, but since it had nowhere to go it returned to the house from which it came and brought more evil spirits with it. The last state was worse than the first. Jesus stated: "When a strong person, fully armed, guards his own palace, his goods are in peace; but when someone stronger comes along he overtakes that person and overcomes him; he takes all that the person trusted in and divides his spoil."

Perhaps it is hard for you and me to imagine demons attacking where we live. But it is true.

The word demon (daimon) is connected with the Greek verb meaning to "tear apart" or "divide." In antiquity the people blamed every influence which tended to tear them apart on demonic invasion. The demons were fallen angels and no one was safe from them. They inhabited the sands of the desert, as well as the depths of the oceans. No place and no time was safe from the things which tore people apart.

Alan Richardson claims, "Christianity conquered the other religions of the ancient world partly because of its success in casting out the fear of demons . . ." Indeed, most of Jesus' miracles were not seen as healings but as power encounters with a declared adversary and enemy.

I suggest to you this evening something we know to be true but perhaps refuse to recognize. There still present in our world forces which "tear apart" and "divide" our households; the devil still goes house-hunting and there are plenty of fallen angels in the world. In fact, sometimes we are fallen angels. Consequently, I suggest that since we are a people possessed with desires that force us into deeds of evil, perhaps we should look again at what the Bible tells us to do when demons attack us and the devil goes house-hunting. It's an area we cannot neglect.

Jesus told this parable about an empty house because the people of his day were living under certain illusions.

Much of our Bible is about how evil uses illusion to move in on people and set up housekeeping. People who live by illusions oftentimes come back to reality with a thud. Adam and Eve in paradise have this illusion that they can be like God. They wind up in the wilderness, kicked out of paradise for good. Their son Cain labors under the illusion that he is inferior to his brother. He winds up a murderer. Abraham, Isaac and Jacob, in the misty dawn of our history, labor under the illusion that they can leave their children set for life with property and money. Their children squander it — every bit of it. The nation, Israel, labors under the illusion that all its problems will be solved if it just has kings like other nations. It winds up under David and Solomon burdened by taxation and split into two nations after a horrible civil war.

Living under an illusion can be a horrible thing. Some of you know that. A student comes in with the illusion that he or she can live cheaper off campus. After a few months of paying deposits for everything from telephone to gas turn on, some high food and utility costs and other unforeseen expenditures, the student learns that just sweeping out one problem doesn't mean that a whole host of new demons won't start tearing you apart.

Then you can get married and really learn that the old adage "two can live cheaper than one" is a complete illusion.

The parable is clear. There is no freedom without responsibility; no deliverance without constant vigilance.

Even today we know Jesus' parable to be true. Consider some of the illusions under which we live. Some people live under the illusion that if we just create better outward conditions then we are free from problems. Outward conditions are important. We have worked hard to clean out some impediments from the past. In some respects we 20th century Americans are the most swept clean generation in history. Independence has been gained for women. Thank God we've swept away those barriers. You women can now almost do anything with your life you want to do. Materialism has increased for us all — we have swept away the demons of lack of gadgets. We have kicked out of our house the immobility and lack of entertainment options which shackled former generations. The automobile, the jet airplane, and new entertainment mediums have kicked out that demon. Supermarkets and gadgets have delivered mother from the house. You'd think our houses would be rather happy places, wouldn't you?

Yet evil still seems to go house-hunting and ushers in even more demons. The automobile and the jet take Mom and Dad away from the home. The new gadgets cost a great deal and both Mom and Dad have to be employed outside the home whether they want to or not. We have "latch keys" on the outside of the door and "latch key" children on the inside of the door. The new entertainment and communication devices also pump a lot of garbage into our homes. The newly-founded materialism crumbles moral values and the lifestyle based on gadgets and independence often turns into the unhappiness of divorce. And you women are now free to experience heart attacks, anxiety, smoking, drinking, lung cancer and high blood pressure. Indeed, you're closing the gap and dying younger as a result of some of these demons that moved in when the old one was swept out.

I don't think this parable about illusions is so remote from our experience as we might think.

How does a person solve this housing problem? Look at the parable. Jesus states that a strong person must guard his or her goods. In other words we must all stand up and take responsibility for the stuff we create. We can't live under the illusion that there's a scapegoat responsible for everything that happens to us. We have to be responsible for our own life.

You might remember that in the ceremony of the atonement in ancient Israel they took a goat, put cloth around his horns and into the cloth were placed the sins of the people. Then the goat was led out into the wilderness, ostensibly carrying the responsibility for the sins and evil with him. The goat was called a scapegoat. Even today when demons attack us, the first response of many is to find a scapegoat on whom all the blame can be placed. That's my most frequent response, I'm afraid. We can find the scapegoats everywhere: the world situation, the neighborhood we live in, the schools we attend, the church, an illness, the television, our heredity, our friends, our teachers, our neighbors. We can indict a few scapegoats. That's an easy sweeping out of the house. Then our conscience grows easy and more demons come rushing in.

Secondly, we cannot labor under the illusion that religious decisions made long ago are going to work for today. Life is a process of constant vigilance. Maybe you did make a nice commitment to religion, values and education as an adolescent. Great! You swept your house clean then, but it won't last forever, if this parable is correct. Maybe you were very close to God, very close to your family, very close to the church, very committed to your values at one time. But now you're going to rest for a while, take a breather from all that "stuff." You'll go back to it later. Right! You'll be good again when you get a career! You'll straighten up then. I doubt it. You see, a house doesn't remain empty. Your life and your values don't stay neutral.

Locate yourself away from sacred music. Locate yourself away from the ideals and ideas in the Christian heritage. Get away from prayer and the symbols of the cross and the resurrection. Locate yourself away from people who at their best are trying to transform their lives and build their characters.

Where is your life going to live? You've got to live somewhere. It's a housing problem of the first order.

What a wonderful parable this is. It has two great meanings for us: *1) we have to be responsible for our own lives every day* and *2) we can't rent ourselves out to other values for a time and then try to go back to our best selves and later find the house empty.*

The World's Best Kept Secret
Matthew 6:25-33
Mark 12:41-44

Our society often paints a very dull picture of being good. It's almost as if wickedness is more interesting than righteousness. We continue to be interested in the Hitler era. Hardly a night passes that two or three cable stations don't have a documentary or a movie about the Adolph Hitler era. Many a theater owner and video store manager have found that the movies rated G and PG certainly do not attract the large audiences that R-rated movies attract. Certainly our medias have found that goodness is not very interesting. Bad news doesn't sell. A person may live 50 years without causing anyone to look around. But if he or she does something *outrageously* bad, the papers and evening news will certainly cover it.

I noticed that the *High Point Enterprise* had a story on the Industrial Services of Guilford County, a work setting for the mentally retarded, having received national recognition for excellence. The story was buried back on page 6B. A few years ago a worker there was charged with sexual misconduct. That story ran on page 1 of the paper, front page, for three consecutive days.

I once did a long, three-hour interview at Harvard with Kathryn Mackin and Karen Evans of ABC for *20/20* and *World News Tonight*. My former classmate and suitemate, David Stockman, was directing the nation's budget. At the time, ABC was putting together a segment on his former life. Now, my wife Diane, in my opinion, has a keen eye for furniture and furnishings. My secretary at the time, Ruiko Conner, was a Japanese woman who was also an artist. To say the least, my office looked very attractive, with Cohasset Colonial furniture and Harvard chairs all over the place. Then the camera crew arrived. After all the cables were laid and the lights set up, I was required to leave my office for an hour. The camera crew "rearranged" the office. When they had finished, it looked like what a weird Ivy League professor's office is supposed to look like. All the plants were gone. Ratty-looking furniture had been pulled in from our storage room and a row of books had been pulled from the shelves and placed all around the floor. It looked cluttered and weird. I heard a cameraman say, "Now, this is more like it."

We concluded the interview outside on Divinity Avenue, by the William James Psychology Building. The cameramen went way down the street with their telescopic lense and boom mike. The weather was frigid. Kathryn Mackin and I stood there shivering, trying to drink coffee and jump up and down to keep warm. Dozens of people, nicely dressed students and natty professors walked past us on their way to classes. "Not yet, not yet," yelled the director. Finally, a high school class from a nearby suburb finished their tour of the Science Museum and poured out into the street. A few of the boys had earrings; some of the girls had the heavy metal attire and dyed orange hair. Half of the group had jamboxes and Walkman units. "Now, now, move it, start walking. Mingle, mingle," yelled the director. "These aren't our students, these aren't our students," I kept saying as we walked and filmed.

The director replied, "No, but they look like what the average American watching television thinks college students look like. It will perk their interests. People will switch the channel if they see men and women in suits and dresses carrying briefcases. It would be boring."

Lest we be unfair to the media, our world of religion often operates under the same premise. I once attended an evangelism conference. It featured "testimonies" from a converted former prostitute from Las Vegas, a murderer who had found Jesus in prison, a former drug dealer from Miami, and a recent convert to Christ from a mental institution. Certainly those testimonies were interesting, if not spellbinding. Who in his or her right mind would fill a convention hall to listen to an unfamous elderly person say, "I have lived a good and faithful life. Christ has been my constant companion since youth and I have quietly but faithfully attended and supported his church all of my adult life." We religious people also tend to give an inordinate amount of space and time to the former vices of our people. There is, indeed, this rather curious notion that wickedness is interesting while goodness is dull. It's almost like being good and the excitement of goodness is the world's best kept secret.

Jesus Christ showed the world that the most fascinating pursuit in the world is that of being good. The finest adventure upon which a person can enter is the quest for goodness and for God. Whatever one might or might not believe about Jesus, one must admit that Jesus made goodness interesting. People followed him about in droves as if he had been leading a circus procession. He picked up worthless beggars off the streets and, by the sheer contagion of his own life, made new people out of them. He told them to be quiet about their conversion. After most of his miracles he said, "Go home; live there as a witness." He walked among self-satisfied prigs, causing them to see and hear what they had never seen or heard before. He came eating and drinking with public officials. His table-talk changed the lives of people. And he elevated to public awareness good people who had faithfully labored in obscurity for decades, even little widows who silently threw in two mites into the offering plate.

This week I went to a video store to look for a movie. The manager told me, "This is a fabulous movie. It's full of action, rated R. It has been out a whole six months, and it's still in the top 12 in rentals." Imagine that. Still in the top 12 after a *whole six months.*

The story of Jesus Christ came out 1,900 years ago, and it is still a best seller. In a world in which gymnasts retire at age 19, a golfer joins the senior tour at age 50, a professional athlete hangs it up at age 35, a best selling novel fades after three years and popular movies wane in two years, there has to be something extremely attractive and interesting about an event and a person that is still a bestseller after 1,900 years.

Goodness can be attractive and interesting. Sometimes that comes as a great shock to people.

I'll never forget a particular revelation that came upon my life. As a child and teenager, I had labored under the assumption that the only way for me to go to college was on a football scholarship. And that's exactly what I set about to accomplish. During my days at Furman, I had a roommate who was extremely studious. I wanted to keep up with him, so I threw myself, with a passion, into every curricular and university service pursuit that he did. One day in my junior year, I went to the office of my history professor to discuss a paper. At the end of the conference he said, "Warlick, I was talking with the dean yesterday, and your grades and activities are such that you could have an academic scholarship if you wanted one. You don't have to play football unless you want to."

Well, it was like somebody hit me between the eyes with a two-by-four. "What? You mean they pay you for good grades? Come on. No. You're kidding. Get off it. Let me get this straight. You mean I can get just as much money by studying as I can out there on the field? You're serious? They pay you to make good grades?"

He went on to explain that you could get scholarships for playing in the band, singing, being good in chemistry — all that stuff. Well, nobody had told me that before or if they had, it never sank in. My goodness, I mean, they pay people to do those things.

Unless you think me a complete rube, let me tell you that for many people that is still a revelation. The young person looks at you with disbelieving eyes when you assert that you can get paid more in life for goodness than for anything else. The notion that if you do not do drugs you wind up, in the long run, with more friends than if you do, seems strange. And many a young woman cannot comprehend the notion that if you enter marriage as a pure person, as one who is not well-experienced in casual sex, that you are more attractive and interesting to members of the opposite sex. It still comes as a revelation. The idea that in terms of relationship with God, genuine friendships and personal fulfillment, you get paid back more in life when you dutifully and faithfully try to live a quiet, loyal life in Christ than when you do not, is still quite a shock to people.

Jesus told a story one day about a certain poor widow who rather naturally and unassumingly approached the treasury of the synagogue. She quietly cast in all that she had. Although the amount was far less than others had given out of their abundance, she was the only person who seemed not to be playing a part. She was the only one who gave out of her natural goodness. The others gave out of their concern how they might look to others.

You know how that goes. Many people go to symphony concerts not because they like classical music but because they know they ought to like it, and it is the proper thing for a person of their position to be seen at the symphony. In like manner, many of us belong to civic groups not because we like civic clubs but because we ought to like them, and it is the proper thing for a person of our position to belong to a civic club. Some people actually go to church because they feel they owe it to their family and their position to be in church. A few even privately stand up and thank God they are not like those who do not attend.

This poor widow came and gave because she was a part of life's greatest adventure. She was simply doing what she felt she was created to do. The greatest adventure in the world is goodness and the kingdom of God, because that's what we were made to do.

Jesus called attention to the beauty and the interesting aspects of people and things doing what they were made to do. He spread his hands out over the fields. "Look at the lilies of the field," he said. "They neither toil nor spin. They do the things they were made to do. They are so attractive and so beautiful because they reach out and claim all they were meant to claim from the sun, the rain, the soil and the dew. They are truly clothed with beauty."

"Do that," Jesus said. "Do the things you were made to do. Seek you first the kingdom of God and its goodness and you will be beautiful, too."

If I read Jesus correctly, God did not sit down and say, "I need to create some men and women. I need human beings. We need to create a planet where some people can snort drugs, make money off one another, hoard the resources of a planet to themselves, and see how many people of the opposite sex they can bed, wed and take advantage of." Rather, God said, "The greatest thing in the world is love and goodness. I'll create a place where people can learn that, a place where people can be in my own image, a place where people can learn that this goodness is the most attractive, fulfilling and interesting thing in the world."

Jesus Christ and many of the good men and women who have lived and died in the life of this college, their church and among good friends, have shown us that the most attractive and interesting pursuit in the world is goodness. That may indeed be the world's best kept secret. Don't miss out on it!

Survival And The Self

Coping With Anger In A Close-up World
Repairing Your Broken Dreams
Don't Give Up Too Soon!
Wheels Instead Of Walls
The Shortest Distance Is Not A Straight Line

Coping With Anger In A Close-up World

Ephesians 4:25-32
Matthew 20:20-24

A volcano is a very tall mountain until it blows its top. Some people are that way as well. I'm one of them. I speak to you this evening as a top blower. The subject of anger intrigues me. One week I was enjoying a cup of coffee with some friends. We were discussing our various work plans for the weeks ahead, and I casually mentioned that I would have to make certain that we removed all the politicians' campaign signs from the yard of the church I pastored. It is a voting place and not all the signs get removed by the people who place them there. One of the landowners spoke up and said, "Well, nobody better stick a sign in the yard of one of my rental properties." A politician in our group spoke up and said, "If I had the permission of the tenant I'd sure stick one in the ground." In a loud voice the former replied, "Yea, and I'd rip it out and throw it on your front doorstep, too." The other retorted, "Well, if you did, I'd pick it up and bash your head in with it." The discussion went downhill from even that level. Can you imagine the best of friends saying these things? Of course you can. Anger. We never know where it will crop up next in our lives.

Our world is a world that has to live close-up with the people in it. More and more of our people live on less and less of the land. Close-up living creates problems. Watch a family with children as they depart from their automobile following a six-hour drive. Examine the family that has spent a week in a motal room or a small condo at the beach. Look at the faces of the people who disembark from a jetliner after an overseas flight. See the man who has just spent three days at a conference with his boss. Look at the facial expressions of the parents of freshmen. How sad they are. Some even hang around a few days after orientation is over. We hardly ever see the parents of upperclassmen. They're glad to have you back in school, and you're glad to be here.

It is not easy to be forgiving and kind in our kind of world. We all need space, and it is becoming harder to find. Our grandparents had lots of room. Agriculture was the primary method by which people earned a living. They could do pretty well as they pleased on their property. Heck, they did not even have to lock the doors. When you got mad at my Uncle Jack's farm, Mother just ran you outside to walk through the tobacco or corn fields until you cooled off. You didn't have to worry about being hit by a car or having someone try to kidnap you or sell drugs to you. Then, when you had cooled off, grandparents, parents, cousins, aunts and uncles, living in fairly close proximity, gave you a wide area over which to spread your feelings.

Our world is a lot more close-up. We live house to house, apartment to apartment, and townhouse to townhouse. We drive fender to fender. We work elbow to elbow. And we here at High Point College go to a small enough school where we know almost everybody. We often get in each other's way. And when we try to spread out our feelings, we often find that the larger family is no longer there to absorb them. We have to focus our anger on fewer people. It naturally becomes more intense.

Living close-up has problems. We all love and hate the very people with whom we are the closest. The two feelings exist side-by-side.[1] All of us compete with one another for honors and recognition, and if we do not get them we become angry. We compete for power, and if we do not acquire it, more anger is generated. Fathers and sons compete with one another, and daughters and mothers compete with each other. We live in a competitive democracy.

Consider Jesus. Like most of us, he found it easier to be a star in other places than in his own hometown. And he found it easier to accomplish great physical and medical feats than to remove anger from his own closest friends. Here was a man, the Son of God, who could calm an entire sea in the middle of a raging storm and tell a leper he was healed. Yet, as our Scripture for today indicates, he could not prohibit a jealous woman from making an idiotic statement or keep the other 10 disciples from getting angry at her two boys. That's life, isn't it? We can often run a business or recover from surgery or complete a great service project or make the dean's list easier than we can dissipate our feelings of anger towards those closest to us.

Consequently, the person who cannot cope with anger in close-up relationships is going to be an alienated person in our kind of world. "One of the very difficult tasks in growing up is that of accepting that we are not the axis around which everyone and everything revolves, that there are other people who are interested in themselves and are not particularly interested in us."[2]

How do we cope with that? Big question! Fortunately our Scriptures provide much focus and clarity on the problem of anger. There are some religious helps to guide us.

In the first place, we can recognize the tremendous harm we do to ourselves through being angry. E. Stanley Jones once reminded a person that "a rattlesnake, if cornered, will sometimes become so angry that it will bite itself." That is exactly what the harboring of hate and resentment against others is: a biting of oneself. We think that we are harming others in holding these spites and hates, but the deeper harm is to ourselves.[3]

What happens to us when we get angry? Hate pumps up our blood pressure. More sugar pours into our system. The heart beats faster. More adrenalin is secreted to dilate the pupils of the eyes, and chemical changes occur in the blood. Even tissue changes take place. In fact, a good optometrist will not examine the eyes of an angry person. You see, anger distorts the retina through abnormal blood flow. Consequently, it is correct to say that a person who is angry most of the time is a sick person.

Jesus and the Scriptures were interested in the health of human beings. That is why they talked about anger so much. When Jesus admonished his followers, "Bless them that curse you, pray for them that despitefully use you and persecute you," he wasn't trying to be "far out" or overly dramatic. You see, he was not making the statement for the benefit of others but for our own benefit. In order to be free and healthy, we must pray for those who we think are our enemies. We must channel those emotions into something positive or like the rattlesnake we will bite ourselves to pieces. Anger is a form of energy. We can say "forget it." But no one can do that. Energy cannot be destroyed. It can only be converted into another form of energy. Do you pray for those you are angry at?

Secondly, we must recognize that we love and hate those people who are closest to us. Consequently, *we must never cut ourselves off from those who get in our way and make us mad or we will miss some of life's greatest blessings.* Look at Jesus, for example. Jesus got angry most often at his close disciples. He screamed at Peter and called him "a devil." He became irritated at the whole lot of them at Gethsemane when they all went to sleep on him and then offered the excuse of being tired. He had to keep 10 of them from punching out James and John and probably their mother, also. Compare his great calmness and compassion with outsiders — those whom he healed and forgave. Yet to whom did Jesus return after his resurrection? Not the crowd he fed with fish and bread. Not the woman with the bleeding ulcer or the man with the lame foot. He came back to that bunch of people that he argued with. And who were the people who gave their lives in faith to Jesus? Who wrote the gospels? *There is not a single gospel written by someone Jesus did not get angry at.* Not a single healed person wrote a gospel. Not a single person among the 5,000 on the hillside who witnessed the miracle of the loaves and fishes wrote a gospel. No cleansed leper or healed Samaritan stepped forward to write a gospel, did they? Those who followed and loved Jesus were the ones who lived close-up with him; and those were the ones he occasionally became angry with.

We must not let temporary anger and bitterness rob us of the relationships which mean the most to us. When I see a couple on the brink of a marital separation, arguing and full of anger at each other, I worry less about them than a couple who has lost all energy and emotion. The latter couple is a hopeless cause. At least anger is energy, albeit the wrong kind of energy. That energy has at least the faint hope of being converted into another type of energy. But when the energy is lacking, the closeless is gone. It is easier to tame a wild horse than inject energy into a dead one.

Finally, my friends, consider the wisdom in Jesus' calling of us to be "other" directed — to serve. He or she who gives, really gets. He or she who chooses to keep what he has and not share it, really winds up losing everything in the end.

Look at women. The greatest frustration for a woman is to feel that she is not loved or lovable. That can produce tremendous rage or an unconscious desire on her part to get people to tell her she is lovable. If all she does is hold on to that, she gets along with no one. Her husband isn't loving enough and she is ripe for an affair with anyone who will tell her, however temporarily, that she is lovable. "Tell me I'm lovable," is the universal scream of the angry and burned-out woman. A man, on the other hand, feels the greatest frustration when he feels that he is not a man. The macho cowboys roaming the earth with their expensive cars, sweet young girlfriends and headlong pursuits toward being king of the hill, or whatever, are legion.

Both, in their own inimitable way, are really postures of saying, "Hey, the world, my family, my job, my church, everything was put here to meet my needs, to revolve around me, to make me feel like a lovable woman or a kingly man." It is anger deep down inside when those needs are not met.

Jesus said we were put here for another reason — to serve and to love the world with the same intensity that we love ourselves. Think about it. To love your neighbor as you love yourself — to try to make other men feel as worthy as you would like to feel, to make other women feel as lovable as you would like to be loved — that, said Jesus, is what life is about.

The most critical adjustment we have to make in life is moving from being "pleasure"centered to being "other" centered.

If we do not make that critical shift, we will not only be unChristian, we will also be *miserable and sick.*

All of us are born as babies. All our needs are satisfied. Nothing is required of us in return. An ideal world is necessary for our survival. The infant's every need is satisfied. He screams and Mother feeds him. If his bladder is full he lets go into the diaper. Everything revolves around the infant; he or she is the center of the world. One of the hardest tasks in growing up is accepting that we are not the axis around which everything and everyone revolves. We have to give up the pleasure principle and learn to live by the service principle. The person who is not "other"directed is in trouble. The whole world is not interested in us. Unless we learn to serve others and fit into a kingdom that emphasizes servanthood as greatness, we will continue to accumulate anger without even being aware of it.

Anger and living close-up. Those two aspects of our existence seem to go hand in hand, but there are some ways in which we can cope with the situation. Jesus is so right. Anger can consume us and wreck our own health if we do not *convet that energy into praying for those who despitefully use us;* we must *not cut ourselves off from those we are angry with or we will miss some of life's finest blessings; and we must make a critical adjustment from being pleasure centered to being other centered.*

May God help and bless all of us as we cope with anger in close-up relationships.

---

1. Leo Madow, *Anger: How to Recognize and Cope with It* (New York: Charles Scribner's Sons, 1972), p. 20.

2. *Ibid*, p. 29.

3. Jones, as quoted in Robert G. Tuttle, *Help Me, God! It's Hard to Cope* (Lima, Ohio: C.S.S. Publishing Co., 1981), p. 23.

Repairing Your Broken Dreams
Luke 24:13-24
Romans 8:28-30

Dreams and visions are important in life. Every action we take in life was designed by someone. Every piece of clothing, every building, every hymn book, every chair, every light fixture, and every automobile existed first in someone's vision. Someone had to have the idea or the dream to turn out the product. The same holds true for the way we act. As Jesus said, "The eye is the seat of the body." If you cannot dream it, cannot envision it, then you simply cannot do it.

Dreams and visions can also be very crushing. Not all dreams come true. We invent certain images of ourself, certain pictures of the way life is supposed to be and then we are somewhat shocked at the way things do not turn out.

Dr. J. Wallace Hamilton, in his book *Horns and Halos in Human Nature*, tells of one of the weirdest auctions in history. It was held in the city of Washington, D.C. It was an auction of designs, actually patent models of old inventions that did not make it in the marketplace. There were 150,000 designs up for auction. There was an illluminated cat to scare away mice. There was a device to prevent snoring which consisted of a trumpet reaching from the mouth to the ear. One person designed a tube to reach from his mouth to his feet so that his breath would keep his feet warm as he slept. There was an adjustable pulpit which could be raised or lowered. You could hit a button and make the pulpit descend or ascend to dramatically illustrate a point. Obviously, at one time somebody had high hopes for each of those designs which did not make it.[1] Some died in poverty, having spent all of their money trying to sell their dream. One hundred fifty thousand broken dreams! Is there anything sadder?

If we call God the master designer of the universe, then we must view the New Testament as a book of broken dreams. It begins with a massacre of innocent children by King Herod. It is centered in the execution of its hero. And it ends with the martyred saints crying, "How long, O Lord, how long?" The crucifixion of Jesus caused serious questions to be posed in the minds of humanity. There on the cross was a man who loved his enemies, a man whose righteousness was greater than the Pharisees, a man who was rich but became poor, a man who gave his robe to those who took his cloak, a man who prayed for those who despitefully used him.[2] Yet, society crucified him, executed him. The question to ask in the presence of this awesome scene is whether such goodness is the design of the universe or forms an exception. Is life designed to be loving, serving, giving and dying? Does that design work? Does it pay off? Is it rewarding?

We perhaps can identify with the men on the road to Emmaus who were walking and talking with each other. They told of all that had happened, how this Jesus of Nazareth, mighty in deed and word before God and all the people, had been condemned to death and crucified.

Are there any clearer words of a broken dream than theirs? "But we had hoped he was the one to redeem Israel (Luke 24:21)." Oh, we had hoped he was the one to make it. We had dreamed he would be the one. But it just didn't work out.

All of us have dreams for ourselves and our lives that just do not make it. We come back home on the Emmaus road with our dream broken in our hip pocket, a sure-fire program that fell flat, a preventive that didn't prevent, a solution that did not solve, a panacea that did not pan out. We wail the plaintive cry, "But we had hoped this would redeem us. Oh, we had hoped it would be another way." St. Paul wrote to the Romans. He told them that he hoped to see them on his way to Spain. Going to Spain was his grand design, his great dream, his high hope. But Paul never got to Spain. Instead, his journey ended in a prison cell in Rome. He could not pull off what he saw in his mind.

It has been very well said that *every person dreams of one life and is forced to live another.* Such appears to have been true for Jesus, and yes, even for God! From the Garden of Eden to the crucifixion, God seems to have had a grand dream for the human race but was forced to live another. Every person dreams of one life and is forced to live another.

For example, Jacob Martinson is president of High Point College. Jacob Martinson had a dream that one day he would be a college president. But unless I'm wrong, when he got to be a college president he found that it wasn't at all like he'd dreamed it would be. He dreamed of one kind of life as a college president and then was forced to live another kind of life.

Gart Evans is dean of students. Gart probably had a dream that one day he'd be a dean. He had in his mind what the life of a dean of students would be like. Bet it didn't turn out exactly the way he thought it would.

Parents have dreams for their children. We all do. I always knew my children could be a cross between Albert Einstein, Tom Selleck and Bo Jackson. On the other hand, I'm certain that I'm not their dream of a parent, either. I knew just how I'd be as a parent in my dreams. I'd be slim, popular, handsome and very caring and understanding. I'd be up on their music, and kind and tolerant when they brought home poor grades. I'd spend hours communicating with my boys. We'd go down the road, arm-in-arm like Andy Taylor and Opie in Mayberry on the way to the fishing hole and have these long, meaningful father-son talks. You dream one life and are forced to live another.

College can be that way. Everyone had a dream of what college would be like. Mid-term grades are soon to be out and I'm certain a few students will go limping home on the Emmaus road with some broken dreams in their hip pockets.

Here, it seems, is the essence of life. If indeed every person dreams of one life and is forced to live another, then the manner in which one repairs that dream has to be the greatest news in the world. The essence of the crucifixion and the resurrection of Jesus Christ is not solely to be found in a personal guarantee of life after death for you and me. The resurrection of Christ is an affirmation of a certain dream for life. The schematic designs of human evil were exposed and condemned for what they were. The central claim of the New Testament is the ultimate triumph of goodness. The resurrection is the triumph of a design for life that is upheld as the fundamental principle of the universe even if the world tries to crucify it.

Consequently, Paul could affirm, "And we know that all things work together for good to them that love God, to them who are called according to his dream (Romans 8:2)." Here Paul is not saying that we all get to live the life of our dreams. A lot of things happen to us that are not good. We are indeed forced to live another kind of life at times. Paul is saying that if a person will consider all the experiences of his or her life, both the good and the bad, and bond them together with love for God, then the sum total of that life, the grand design of that person's history will be good. As such, it is indeed possible to believe in the sun when it is not shining, to believe in love when you cannot directly feel it, and to believe in God when God is silent for a period. Even if the world crucifies you, the design of God's universe and your life with it will ultimately triumph. The dream will triumph even if it is not immediately evident.

Sometimes it is important for us to back up from our particular experiences, hurts, angers and pressures to reflect on the grand design of things, the larger issues. Perhaps that is why the first gospel, Mark, was not written in finished form until almost 100 years after Jesus died and rose. Perhaps only then could the early church feel strong enough to assert that the design of love holds, stands, triumphs for all generations over the design of darkness and death.

You and I live by our dreams as much as by our particular experiences. In this world of broken dreams, in this world where we dream of one life and are forced to live another, a conclusion comes from resurrection. If God's dream for goodness triumphs, then one thing is certain.

Failure is relative to time. No one really knows when he has succeeded or failed if all he does is look at the present.[3] God's design and God's time turn a lot of failures into successes. We must measure success by God's standard of design in history, not whether or not we are immediately on the top of the world's heap. I know many people who have "arrived" and they are notn very happy. I know others who look back on what they thought was a burden at the time and they now view it as having been a tremendous learning experience.

Consider Rev. Kiyoshi Tanimoto. In 1944, he was the minister of the largest Protestant congregtion in southern Japan. It was in the city of Hiroshima. Tanimoto must have been proud of his large church. Then one day, a yellow flash came. Mr. Tanimoto dove instinctively into a garden and wedged himself between two huge rocks. A powerful blast of wind and fire blew over him. It knocked him unconscious. When he came to and got on his feet, the city was flat as a desert. Sixty-eight thousand human beings were killed instantly. Only 30 members of his 3,500-member church were still alive. Rev. Tanimoto began to rebuild his crucified church. He arranged for the spiritual adoption of 500 Hiroshima orphans by North American families. As a result of his work, all bomb survivors became eligible for free medical treatment. Rev. Tanimoto also created a Peace Foundation. In that Foundation's museum a little girl named Sadako placed two cranes made of folded paper. It was her belief that if a person who was ill made these little paper cranes, the person would get better. Well, Rev. Tanimoto died and little Sadako also died, after 10 years of horrible suffering.[4] Two people who loved their enemies, whose righteousness was greater than the Pharisees, who were executed by forces they did not understand, cause us to ask, "Where was the design in all of this?" What happened to the dream? They believed in the sun when all they saw was a mushroom cloud that rose six miles high in only eight minutes. They believed in love when they could not feel it, and they believed in God when God was silent for a period. Naked, bleeding, hairless and with skin hanging loose, they went to their early graves. They dreamed of one life and were forced to live another.

Today, 30 years after their death, a statue stands in Hiroshima. The statue was built in memory of their deaths. It is the figure of two children on either side and another child on top, their arms outstretched to express their hope for a peaceful world. For more than 30 years, to this very day, Japanese children keep the center of that statue filled with many-colored paper cranes. God's design of love holds. It stands. It triumphs for all generations over any design of darkness and death. Paul is absolutely correct. History has proved it in a thousand ways. If a person will consider all the experiences of his life and bond them together with love for God, then the sum total of that life will be good.

The design of God will ultimately triumph. From Bethlehem to Gethsemane to Calvary, the innocent do suffer. The good and the lonely often get what they do not deserve. But goodness never stays in the dark. The truth never stays crucified. The central theme in human history is the same as the central theme of the New Testament: *the ultimate triumph of goodness.* If we would but believe that, our lives would claim an unbelievable power and freedom. To believe in that goodness. To believe in the power of your own life through God. That's the first step in repairing a broken dream.

---

1. As used by Charles L. Allen in *The Miracle of Hope* (Old Tappan, New Jersey: Fleming H. Revell Co., 1983), pp. 16-17.

2. See John Howard Yoder, *The Politics of Jesus* (Grand Rapids, Minnesota: William B. Eerdmans, 1972), p. 61.

3. Ernest A. Fitzgerald, *How To Be A Successful Failure* (New York: Atheneum, 1978), pp. 6-8.

4. As told by Bruce McLeon, *City Sermons* (Burlington, Ontario, Canada: Welch Publishing Company, 1986), pp. 69-71.

Don't Give Up Too Soon!
Acts 15:36-40
2 Timothy 4:11

These are very exciting times in which to live. Eastern Europeans in communist countries are enjoying freedoms they have waited for, for 30 years. Nelson Mandela is free after 27 years of being in prison in South Africa. Perhaps it's hard for us to comprehend the faith and the hope which sustained these people for so long. Why didn't they give up sooner? Why not just accept failure, quit, drop out, transfer somewhere else, hang it up?

One of my joys in life was visiting the famous Rijksmuseum in Amsterdam. I had not anticipated that it would be a joy at all. I know little about art. Most of the art appreciation classes I took in college were taught by little men who wore bow ties and plaid coats with striped pants, and droned incessantly in monotone voices. And the day we got off the train at Central Station in Amsterdam had not started well. We went to a restaurant. The Dutch people allow their dogs into restaurants. So I had had a chicken salad sandwich in a coffee shop with a huge dog up against my legs.

My wife and the other couple with us were not delighted, with my commentary as to what I thought of Amsterdam. At last we walked up the huge steps to the Rijksmuseum. We went through room after room of beautiful paintings. Nice paintings. Old paintings. Boring paintings. Yawn! Then we came to a room with some huge *Rembrandt* paintings. I stopped in amazement at the difference in quality. The great painter left out no aspect of the human experience. In addition to the beauty and symmetry of the human body, he faithfully and meticulously painted the moles, the tiny scars, the dirt under the fingernails, the wear of the years in the corners around the eyes, the wrinkles on the face and even the hardening blood vessels. The pictures seemed to be more alive than the other paintings.

In a vivid sense the Bible is a book that is very much alive. It is the Rembrandt of religious experience because it tells life as it really is, with scars and moles and dirt under the fingernails. It chronicles not just the pious events of religious history, but the bitter dregs of failure that lie temporarily at the bottom of everyone's cup. And well it should. *A God that cannot deal with failure is not much of a God.* No one lives life without some failure. Everyone stumbles and falls at some point along the road.

All we know about the early life of Jesus, from the time he was born until the time he began his ministry at age 30, is that he ran away from home when he was 12 years old. For three long, anxious days Mary and Joseph looked for him in vain. Imagine your child disappearing for three days.

The talk among the neighbors must have been quite lively. Mary and Joseph must have faced no small amount of public embarrassment in the experience. What kind of father loses his kid for three days? What kind of a mother loses her boy?

When they were finally able to catch up with him, he was in the temple. They were, understandably, quite angry. Yet, Jesus seemed almost totally unconcerned. "Why have you come after me?" he questioned. "Did you not know I must be here in my Father's house (Luke 2:49)."

The Scriptures relate that Mary and Joseph did not understand at all what their son did or the remarks he made. I can conjecture the modern-day parental and spousal wrath that would have been the response from many. The battle to save self esteem would have been a neurotic categorical demand that the failure was somebody else's fault. "Well, if you weren't gone all the time, Joseph, and spent more time with the boy, he might not prefer these strangers to his own family."

"Well, what kind of homemaker gets so wrapped up in her civic responsibilities and her bridge club, Mary, that she loses the whereabouts of her own child?"

"Well, if you'd go to church more, Joseph, and had finished college, you might be able to answer his religious questions. You dummy!"

Actually, the Scripture simply says that Mary, "his mother kept all these things in her heart." Wouldn't you love to know what those things were? Moles. Warts. Wrinkles. The dirt under the fingernails. Failure. Fortunately she did not give up too soon on him.

In like manner, this Rembrandt of a book we treasure tells of a tremendous family fight that took place in the life of the early church. The first missionary journey of Paul was a glowing success. Paul and Barnabas had literally opened up the world for advancement of the faith. They had planted churches in strategic places. It must have been a hectic pace. Paul was the numero uno champion of Christianity — educated in Tarsus University — a brilliant mind, a powerful tongue and an indefatigable spirit. And Barnabas was equally powerful and brilliant. He was the chief preacher in the church at Antioch where the word "Christian" was used for the first time. He was the man in charge. When Paul was converted no one at Jerusalem headquarters believed it, Barnabas was the one who had presented Paul. Barnabas was somebody. When famine swept Jerusalem, Barnabas had brought money down from Antioch to feed Peter, James and John. And when Peter came out of jail he had nowhere to go, so Barnabas arranged for Peter to stay with Barnabas' sister, Mary, and her boy, John Mark.

Now can you imagine an 18-year-old young person traveling with two racehorses like Paul and Barnabas? They moved fast. They threw their money and power around like they were limitless. The food was bad. But they pressed from one continent to another and traveled through rough seas and dark mountain passes. The mosquitoes were everywhere. And Paul and Barnabas didn't mind going to jail now and then if it would get more publicity for the cause.

Imagine traveling with those two egomaniacs! Well, John Mark had to travel with them. He was Barnabas' nephew.

Perhaps his sister, Mary, persuaded them to take him. Perhaps the young man volunteered out of genuine passion for Christ, but also out of naivete over what it would be like. John Mark failed. He did not finish the journey. He quit. He gave up. He packed up and went home to Jerusalem and to his mother, Mary. He was a young failure in life. A career that never got off the ground. Paul did not like it. When John Mark asked to go on the second journey, Paul flatly said, "No, you're fired. No, you can't go. You're a failure. You quit on me once and you won't get a second chance."

Well, thus began a historic quarrel that became a disaster. The difference between Paul and Barnabas became so sharp that Paul took Silas and headed in one direction and Barnabas and Mark sailed in the other direction to Cyprus. The early church had hardly been planted when its two champions fell out with each other.

I have taken your time to convey these stories because I believe they are there in the Scriptures for a reason: *There are too many people in the world whose lives have been unfulfilled because someone gave up on them too soon!* And there are too many people in the world who gave up on themselves too soon.

Back in the late 1970s, I pastored a church adjacent to Clemson University. Occasionally I would get invited to go over to the football dorm and give a little talk to the players. I continued that practice a few times even after I left South Carolina. On one occasion I was curious about something, so I asked, "How many of you fellows never played organized football before ninth grade in school?" There were 46 athletes in the room and exactly 31 hands went up. Some of the raised hands played in the Super Bowl years later. You see, they were the kids who were too fat, too gangly, too poor or too uncoachable at an early age to play with the smaller kids with finer motor skills. They were the young failures whose frames filled out later, whose baby fat turned into muscle, whose awkwardness came under control later. They were just starting to come into their own while others were peaking.

I repeat, there are too many persons whose lives have been unfulfilled because someone gave up on them too soon.

Fortunately, these biblical stories have a somewhat happy ending. We all know how Jesus and Mary turned out — his passionate concern for her from the cross and his entrustment of her care to John. The story of Paul and John Mark has an equally happy ending. One of the downside risks in being an earthshaker and a traveler is loneliness. When you get out on the point pushing a new idea, it is sometimes lonely out there. And when your cause turns from an immediate success to a minority position in the world, you can find yourself stretched thin beyond your belief. That happened to Paul. In his valiant effort to include the Gentiles in Christianity, his Jewish friends abandoned him. Alone and disconsolate in prison, he wrote these words to the church at Colossae: "Aristarchus my fellow prisoner greets you, and John Mark, the nephew of Barnabas — if he comes to you, receive him and Justus. These are the only men of the circumcision among my fellow workers for the kingdom who have been a comfort to me (Colossians 4:10-11)." Then he wrote to Timothy these words: "Only Luke is with me. Take John Mark and bring him with you; for he is very useful for the ministry (2 Timothy 4:11)."

It is really unbelievable. The rift was healed. The fledgling young disciple filled out. The baby fat turned to muscle and the awkwardness came under control. What a mistake, what a tragic mistake, Paul would have made, giving up on John Mark too soon! As his life wound down, one of the two people who stood by Paul was a person he had fired as a young failure.

There is not a person in this room, if my guess is correct, who does not have at least one person in his or her family, however close or remote, out there trying to find his or her way back from an awful failure. There probably aren't many people here who don't number among their family or former friends or teammates, a John Mark out there trying to find his or her way back from failure. And there will come a time when you will be tempted to give up or quit too soon.

Seven years ago a black woman, a Mrs. Hummings, called me from Winston-Salem. She told me that she had moved there two years earlier from Georgia so her little boy could study in the North Carolina School of the Arts. He played the viola. His mother explained that her son had never played before a live audience. She wondered if we would let him do a concert in our church to get some experience since he had to go to Washington and audition for some financial aid. She stated, "We're here with very little besides a dream for him. We moved the whole family for that dream."

I arranged a time for him to play in Emerywood Baptist Church. Around 60 people turned out to create an audience and help the boy. I'll never forget when he and his mother got out of their car that day over on Country Club Drive. The boy was 13 years old. He was tall and gangly. Awkward looking. He wore tennis shoes and an old felt jacket. He didn't own a suit. And was he shy. But he could play the viola. He was excellent.

After his concert, one of the men in the church came up to me. He said, "We can't let that boy go to audition in Washington in tennis shoes and jacket. He'll be up against well-heeled kids from elite schools. We can at least dress him."

So several of the people collected $400. The next week he and his mother went down to Belks in Weschester Mall. He got two suits and a pair of shoes. A person later commented, "That's a wasted $400. You might as well kiss that off. You'll never see any return on that. What a waste."

Two days ago I received a surprise letter in the mail. It contained a letter from these people I had not heard from in seven years. Enclosed was a newspaper article clipped from *The Winston-Salem Journal*. The headline read "Winston-Salem Musician Is Chosen to Play at Carnegie Hall." Underneath the tuxedo clad picture of that former tennis-shoed 13-year-old was a single sentence: "A dream come true."

So if the Bible says anything to you, it says, "Don't give up too soon!"

Wheels Instead Of Walls
Ezekiel 1:15-19
Acts 10:34-38

Rachel Dunn, the director of the Central High School Show Choir is a distant cousin of mine. Cousin Rachel is also in charge of the Warlick family reunion each summer. Reunions are a lot of fun. They can also be quite awkward.

One feels especially awkward attending the reunion of a family to which one did not belong but simply married into. The same holds true for high school and college reunions. Most of you will marry someone who did not attend your high school Many of you will marry someone who did not attend High Point College. You and your spouse, to keep the peace, will go to another school's reunion.

My wife, Diane, and I journeyed to Augusta, Georgia, one summer to attend her high school class reunion. We waited patiently in a long registration line at the Holiday Inn. They had a little booth set up by the swimming pool. Each member of the class was given a yellow name tag with his or her high school picture affixed to it. The spouses, me included, were given a white name tag with no picture on it. There we were — the yellow badges and the white badges. The yellow badges all ran up to each other and hugged and screamed with delight. The yellow badges told old stories. The yellow badges remembered classrooms and buildings and events.

Needless to say we white badges slowly drifted to the lobby. I could understand them being partial to the yellow badges. It was their place, their school. But it was still awkward being made to feel an outsider to an experience. *They had every right to play favorites.* But it's still an awkward feeling not to be a "favorite."

One of the first things a person learns in adulthood is that our world plays "favorites." The world is a place that exhibits a great deal of partiality. Those who pay the most money get the best seats! Those who occupy the highest positions get the best parking places. Ours is a world of preferential treatment for preferred persons. Some play by one set of rules while others have to play by a different set. It's part of our existence and the greater the responsibility a person has, the better the "perks" that person has. It's a fact of life, and a justifiable one, I think. After all our world revolves around big donations, preferred customers and partial treatment. There are certain fences in life that you and I will never be able to climb over.

After you leave here, it will happen to some of you with your own alma matter, High Point College. It does to all of us. Shortly after our family moved to High Point, I received an invitation in the mail from my college alma mater, Furman University. My name was embossed in gold on an invitation to attend a football game. The packet contained all manner of beautiful brochures, bumper stickers and notebooks, with the college logo on them. Choice seats were being reserved for me at the game. All we had to do was notify the development office when we were going to attend. Frankly, I was shocked. Usually I have to scramble to get a ticket past the five yard line.

A few nights later Diane received a telephone call from Furman. I heard her laughing in the kitchen so I went in to eavesdrop on the conversation. The last words I heard her say were, "No, he isn't that kind of a doctor." You see, in Massachusetts Diane worked as a secretary for Pediatric Associates in Walpole. Somehow the Furman computer had scrambled together her job, my work address in High Point, and my name. I retrieved the packet from the shelf in the utility room and only then noticed the address: "Dr. Harold Warlick, Pediatric Associates, 1300 Country Club Drive, High Point, North Carolina." The poor computer. It thought it had really targeted a preferred alumnus. Needless to say, we haven't received any more special invitations. The development office found out I was a preacher instead of a pediatrician.

I understand it. We live in that kind of world. I benefit from it as well as sometimes become the victim of it. It's nice to occasionally be given partiality. *Our world invented the wall long before it invented the wheel.*

Imagine believing that God plays favorites, too. Israel did. She believed that God was the God of Jews who lived in Jerusalem, worshiped at the temple in Jerusalem and visited all the holy places. God was tied to the land, the place where she lived — the promised land. Everyone who lived there was blessed by God. They were all yellow badge types — kissing and hugging each other and telling stories about Moses and David and all those places that were her sacred past. God lived within the walls of that nation and one day after death there would be a grand reunion of all those yellow badges in that place. God would play favorites forever. God had promised that to them.

Imagine their utter horror when their yellow badges were snatched right off their lapels. Their land was invaded and decimated. Their alma mater was destroyed, its buildings pulled down. They found themselves strangers in a strange land. They were far from home living as outsiders in a strange yet wonderful country called Babylon.

They felt as if their God, their heritage, their worth and their values were walled up far away back where they used to live.

In that critical moment of history the prophet Ezekiel had a vision. He saw living creations. Beside each creature was a wheel. Each wheel seemed to intersect another wheel. When the living creatures rose, the wheels rose. If the creatures faced north, south, east or west, the wheels went in that direction.

What a tremendous vision about the ability of God to move where the human creatures go. To a people who believed God was found within the walls of an ark, or a temple, or a city, or a nation, this was a shocking revelation. God doesn't have a favorite place, a favorite building, or a favorite form. Ezekiel saw wheels instead of walls. God could move.

It's no wonder the slaves in our country in the 18th and 19th century felt such joy and close presence of God as cut off from their native land and even their families they sang "Ezekiel Saw the Wheel."

I think perhaps all of us need to see the wheel more often. We are born into a certain home with a certain religious preference. And it's good that we are. I was born in South Carolina within the walls of a Baptist house and a Baptist wall of faith. If God were confined within the walls of my childhood then I would be in deep trouble right now. If God played favorites I'd either be out of luck in this place or else the most arrogant, pompous, narrow-minded religious cuss you've ever seen. But I did figure out that God's wheels roll beyond the walls of my childhood.

I'm always amazed by the haunting words that came from Peter's mouth in Acts 10: "And Peter opened his mouth and said, 'Truly I believe that God shows no partiality, but in every nation any one who fears him and does what is right is acceptable to him.' "

God does not have favorites. God does not play favorites. God is an impartial God. If we are brutally honest with ourselves we must admit that that's hard to take. The idea that God doesn't play favorites has always been a bitter pill for religious people to swallow. I guess that's one reason why we preachers preach so many lightweight sermons on self-help, personal happiness, individual depression and the book of Revelation with its emphasis on our Christian revenge. Maybe that's why we have so many bumper-stickers and lapel pins with slogans like "God is my co-pilot" or "In case of rapture this car will be unoccupied" while we dodge the tough issues like maybe all those sinners who didn't behave as well as we did will also make it to heaven.

Peter's words and actions hurt some Jewish Christians. They had built some walls around their God. But Peter saw wheels instead of walls.

Peter dared to baptize a Roman, a Gentile. Peter had been "religious" only three years. Yet he presumed to set aside

2,000 years of time-honored tradition and eat with this Gentile, this scum, this outcast, this sleaze-bag. How could he do that? The angry crowd demanded an answer. "How could you do that?"

Peter opened his mouth and said: "Truly I perceive that God shows no partiality. God does not play favorites. God can move around."

J. B. Phillips once said that *the most personal issue you can engage in is what you think God's like.* He contends that quite a number of us have much too small an idea of God. Most people develop a great deal physically, mentally and psychologically as they grow up. They learn their job and become proficient in it. They learn to be a parent and even a grandparent. But, says Phillips, "as far as religion is concerned a lot of them haven't grown up at all."[1]

All of us need to begin to get a few grown-up ideas about God. He cannot be confined to the Baptist or Methodist or Catholic persuasion. He cannot even be confined to this world alone. He cannot be confined to the pages of the Bible, though he speaks there. God cannot be confined to the four walls of a church, though he is present there. God cannot even be confined to the Milky Way.

Ezekiel saw the wheel. Jesus saw the wheel. Peter saw the wheel. It is a great day, a great day indeed, when you and I begin to see the wheels instead of the walls. So be it!

---

1. J. B. Phillips, *Plain Christianity* (London: Epworth Press, 1954), p. 37.

The Shortest Distance Is Not A Straight Line

Matthew 8:5-13; 12:9-13

None of us relishes complications. We want issues to be simple. But now the freshmen are no longer freshmen — they've got four months under their belts in college. Rush week is over so some are now in fraternities and sororities. Faculty are complaining that second term has been just as rushed and frantic as the first. Dr. Warlick isn't new anymore. People are used to Wednesday nights instead of Sunday mornings as the time for worship. Attendance patterns and the reasons for them become more ambiguous. None of us relishes ambiguity — the state where things can have more than one meaning. We want issues to be clear — good or bad. We like the definite "yes" or the definite "no" — truth or lie. We've been at this knowledge game long enough to know there are a lot of "ifs" and "maybes" in life. I was present when a graduate student in history came back from Chapel Hill to Furman for homecoming. He verbally tore into his former history professor. "Before I came to this place and studied under you," he declared, "life was very clear and simple. I knew clearly what was right and wrong, good or bad, truth or falsehood. I came from a small family in a small town. I knew enough, I thought. But you made me complicated. You pointed out all these ambiguities and contradictions in history and religion. And I can't go back to being simple anymore."

Ambiguity is indeed a real problem in life. When a person moves beyond a certain plateau in life, ambiguity is there waiting.

Our parents taught us right and wrong as total absolutes. They had to do that. In childhood few of us could handle ambiguity. *Our teachers got us started in math by teaching us that the shortest distance between two points is a straight line.*

We needed that data base at that time. We were hardly ready for calculus and Einstein in the fourth grade. Then we moved up to a different level of reality and discovered that because of the curvature of the earth, the shortest distance is a curved line, not a straight one.[1] No airplane would attempt to fly to Europe in a straight line. It would be too far. You either take the circle route by Iceland and Northeastern Canada or you stay home.

The apostle Paul spoke of this: "When I was a child, I spoke as a child; when I became an adult, I reached a new plane of thought." Before Paul became a Christian, his life was fairly simple. He knew, he thought, the clear right and the obvious wrong. Amazingly enough, after he gave his life to Christ things got more, not less complicated. He encountered ambiguity. The farther he traveled the worse it became. He started saying things like, "We look through a clouded glass and only see things dimly. We are certain of Christ, but in the meantime, until he makes all things clear in his kingdom anew, we prophesy in part and speak in part. We just don't know everything."

There are, of course, certain religious statements which avoid ambiguity: "Jesus Christ, the same yesterday, today and tomorrow!" No ambiguity in that. People pack auditoriums and television studios to hear charismatic leaders give clear answers about right and wrong. Religious empires are built. If a person can promise to separate life between what is real and false, right and wrong, the masses will give that person their money, their allegiance and their devotion. It's a natural inclination. Can you imagine Paul standing in such a place and going out over the airwaves with, "I prophesy in part and I speak in part. I see the truth like a man looking through a foggy windowpane. I just don't know everything." Well, he would not be on the air very long. People want a straight line. That's the shortest distance to God, is it not?

What does it take to evoke a response from God? Does it take a gallon of faith? A pound? An ounce?

In the account of the healing of the centurion's servant, a *huge amount* of faith brings a healing. Jesus healed the servant long distance because ". . . 'not even in Israel have I found such faith' (Matthew 8:10)." Here it would seem that the formula is one gallon of faith equals a cure.

But at another time, Jesus said that if we have faith the size of a mustard seed we can move mountains. Here it would seem that an ounce of faith is the magic ingredient in the formula.

Yet in other encounters, Jesus worked miracles when faith did not exist at all. A man in the synagogue had a withered hand (Matthew 12:9-13). Scripture doesn't tell us if the man had ever heard of Jesus or had any faith in him at all. Scripture maintains that the man never asked to be healed. Jesus simply healed the man. Here it would seem that no faith at all is required for Jesus' work.[2]

What is the magic formula? What determines when God shall act and when God shall not act? Certainly God is not whimsical or moody. There must be a better explanation.

I think Jesus and Paul evidenced to us that *ambiguity is a reality in life and we do ourselves more harm by trying to avoid it than by embracing it.*

I don't like being complicated. I don't like ambiguity. I like my religion straight. But sometimes straight isn't the shortest distance to God and truth. I wish that he had just separated the sheep and goats on the earth instead of mixing them all in together until the afterlife. I wish he had simply given us a formula and said, "Apply this. These are from Satan and these are from God. Here is evil and here is good." Instead, he left us that parable about the wheat and the weeds growing together in the same field — good and evil both flourishing in the same ground. I wish it were like tonight's basketball game where the home team wears the white jerseys and the visiting team the colored jerseys. At least you'd known whom to pull for. Instead, life's often like a scrimmage between the same team with the same color uniforms. You often have to run the play and set it in motion, then see who's coming to defend or advance.

Ambiguity is a reality in life. There is never a formula for God. The Old Testament records show that sometimes God waits to act until he sees our faith and sometimes he acts where we can observe no faith at all. God is God. We have difficulty squeezing God into a formula to write on a tract or religious blackboard and apply every time we have a problem. If there were a set formula as to prayer, daily readings or particular appeals, then the early church would have left us a little pamphlet with that formula on it, instead of this Bible which is exactly 1,303 pages long.

Children have died whose parents prayed a great deal. The dead are strewn across the battlefields of a hundred wars — the dead for whom millions of parents and spouses wept. Mothers and fathers have died in a thousand different ways. Trouble, tragedy and defeat move among us. One group will say that such is God's will. Another group calls it Satan. Another group says Divine power doesn't work.

The simple truth of all faith is that we are not God. We are humans. There are things we may not know for centuries. *Faith is not in what we know, but in what we do not know and yet believe.* There is ambiguity in the world and we cannot play at being God. Yet it does not make sense to turn from God's strength just because there is ambiguity in life. It takes more faith to trust God in the blackest midnight when there appears to be no answer at all than to fit God into a formula.

Jesus has told us that God is a presence in life; that God has triumphed once and for all over evil. Good emerges and evil feeds upon it and destroys. Yet forces we do not understand make use of evil to bring good again. Trust experience, Jesus said, "My power and my presence I leave in this world. Trust your own experience. Trust the tradition of those who have given their lives for the faith."

The great Danish theologian, Soren Kierkegaard, said, "Life can only be understood backwards, but it must be lived forwards." That's true. God reveals himself and his presence not merely in a word on the gilt-edged page of the Bible or in the flutter in some hopped-up religious heart. God is present in the curved line as in the straight line. God is a mysterious presence in time of absence. He does not demand order. God is revealed and present.

That is the history of the God of the Bible. The God of the Bible is different from any god known to humans. In Egypt the belief was in the status quo of the cosmic order. The Pharaoh was the divine head of this cosmic order, the sun god. Everything had a place, a royal line, a formula.

Mesopotamia was a chaotic place. The people there believed that men and women were created evil. So the king, the god, was the one who had the greatest power, the greatest numbers and the most money. You simply learned your place in society and called on the king to help you. There was a formula, a given place for you.

God was made known in a regular pattern. In family life the inheritance was passed on to the oldest son. The most powerful, the most prayerful, the most successful figure was the representative for God. God's presence was there. One did not look for God in the darkest nights of the soul — in ambiguity and tragedy. Wherever God's presence was, it certainly wasn't there.

But look at our God. Abraham experiences a family tragedy. Ishmael is his first-born son. Isaac is the younger half-brother. God promises Abraham that his family will be blessed as a great nation. Ishmael is the first born, the carrier of the family order. But Ishmael is thrown out into the wilderness at the insistence of Abraham's wife, Sarah. Abraham is crushed. Ambiguity settles over him. He doesn't know which way to lean. So God reminds Abraham in this out-of-the-ordinary crisis that his presence will be with both children. God reveals himself right in the midst of something Abraham cannot avoid. Then Isaac marries Rebekah and has twins. Esau is the oldest and, as the one who was birthed first by a few seconds, is supposed to get the blessing and wealth of Isaac. But Jacob, the younger twin, tricks old blind Isaac and snatches his brother's rightful life. Where is God when the formula is broken? Right there. Right there to carry on the promise and bring about an ultimate reconciliation of the twins. Then Jacob is confronted with an ambiguous situation. He works seven years to marry Rachel and is tricked into marrying Leah, the older sister of Rachel. The formula, if there was one, is broken to pieces. Jacob finally gets on track with Rachel, but by then he's had 10 sons by Leah. Rachel finally gives him Joseph but dies in the birth of Benjamin. The death of his wife almost breaks Jacob. Two little boys without their mother. Surely this Joseph and Benjamin will have it rough. The pattern is broken, the order is disturbed, the formula crushed and eradicated beyond recovery. The straight line, short distance to God is snapped. So Rachel, dearly beloved wife of Jacob, is buried in the cemetery beside the road outside a little one-horse town which later was given the name of Bethlehem.

And the one who was born there of her lineage placed his followers in the midst of ambiguity. But he said, "Look for me. I will be there. Do not avoid the complexity of life. I will be revealed and present in it."

A little child stands in front of a gumball machine. It is filled with gum. There are at least seven different colors. He has the dime it takes to operate the machine. He wants a green ball of gum. He trustingly places the dime in the slot and pulls the lever. Out comes a red ball. He did everything right. He had enough money and he believed. The machine let him down. He can't understand. He is angry at the machine. He shakes it violently. He kicks it. He speaks harsh words to it. In tears, he declares that's the last time he'll trust a gumball machine. What he wants doesn't always come rolling out even if he has the correct faith and pulls the proper lever. He gets the red ball because the machine does not have his welfare at heart.[3]

If Jesus taught us anything it should be that God is not a gumball machine. God has our welfare at heart. God is not mindless and impersonal. He is present in the midst of ambiguity. And he loves us too much to expect us to carry the whole load by ourselves. That is why he came to our kind of existence and took the burden off our back and placed it on his.

Sometimes we have to stand in our pulpits and are to point to this presence. Sometimes we have to have the courage to embrace this mysterious presence in ambiguity. We don't have the demand or the opportunity, much less the courage to do it often. But true preaching is not therapy. True preaching is not church management or a reinterpretation of the Bible.[4] True preaching is scary! It is scary, just as life is scary, because there is not a magic formula to preach. There is not even a regular pattern to be handed down. *There is only a presence to be felt, a hand to be placed in our hand.* It is a powerful presence. So be it.

---

1. Thomas Conley, "Some Cooked Fish and a Blessing: Reality in Religion," The Pulpit of Northside Drive Baptist Church, Atlanta, Georgia, April 17, 1988.

2. Arnold Prater, *How Much Faith Does It Take?* (Nashville: Thomas Nelson Publishers, 1982).

3. Will Oursler, *The Road to Faith* (New York: Rinehart & Co., Inc., 1960).

4. David Buttrick, "Preaching in an Unbrave New World." *The Spire,* Vol. 13, No. 1 (Summer/Fall 1988).

www.ingramcontent.com/pod-product-compliance
Lightning Source LLC
Chambersburg PA
CBHW060844050426
42453CB00008B/821